*Power of a Woman Series*

Time is Running Out!

"So teach us to number our days, that we may apply our hearts unto wisdom."
Psalm 90:12

Dr. Cassundra White-Elliott

This book is a work of non-fiction combined with fictitious accounts regarding the character Anastasia. However, the accounts of Anastasia's life are factual accounts from the author's life. All Scripture is from the King James Version of the Holy Bible.

CLF Publishing, LLC.
9161 Sierra Ave, Ste. 203C
Fontana, CA 92335
www.clfpublishing.org

Copyright © 2017 by Cassundra White-Elliott. All rights reserved. No portion of this book may be reproduced, stored in a retrieval system, or transmitted by any form or any means electronically, photocopied, recorded, or any other except for brief quotations in printed reviews, without the prior permission of the publisher.

Cover Design by Senir Design. Contact information- info@senirdesign.com.

ISBN # 978-1-945102-21-9

Printed in the United States of America.

Acknowledgements

Thank you, Holy Spirit for leading and guiding me "each word and each sentence of the way" to completing this book. Without you, it would not have reached your people.

Thank you, Lord for loving us so much that you would send us a word! All glory and honor is given unto your Holy name!

Dedications

This book is dedicated to all who have ever tuned their ear to hear what thus saith the Lord. God has a divinely-inspired plan for our lives, and it is up to us to seek His guidance in order to fulfill it. Don't allow the enemy to come in and steal, kill, and destroy. Resist him, and he will flee from you-
with his "tail" between his legs!

March on, soldier! March on!
Do the work of the Lord, while it is yet day!

Table of Contents

Introduction	7
Chapter One	9
Getting an Understanding	
Chapter Two	15
How Strong is Your Faith?	
Chapter Three	21
Whose Voice Is It?	
Chapter Four	41
Uniquely Designed	
Chapter Five	57
Lord, Order My Steps	
Chapter Six	69
Bringing the Assignment to a Close	
Chapter Seven	77
A New Assignment	
Chapter Eight	89
Closing Thoughts	
The Gift of Salvation	91
References	96

About the Author   97

Other Books by the Author   99

Introduction

Adventure is a built-in component of life. To have an adventure means to engage in unknown and possibly hazardous activities. So, if life is going to be adventurous anyway, why not have an adventure with God?

Do you believe God has need of you?

Do you believe He pre-ordained your life before you departed from your mother's womb?

Do you believe your life was not an accident, but that God has a divine purpose for you?

If you don't believe any of the above, read Acts 10:34, *"Then Peter opened his mouth, and said, Of a truth I perceive that God is no respecter of persons."* Peter realized God is not partial to one person over the next. What He does for one, He can do for another. It doesn't mean He *automatically* will do the same, but He surely can.

Now read Jeremiah 1:5, *"Before I formed thee in the belly I knew thee; and before thou camest forth out of the womb I sanctified thee, and I ordained thee a prophet unto the nations."* Before Jeremiah breathed his first breath, God had assigned a purpose to his life. If God ordained Jeremiah for a specific assignment before he was born, wouldn't He do the same for you? Of course, He would. Otherwise, your very existence would be in vain.

If you do believe God has need of you, then at some point in your life, you must consult God and find out why He created you and for what you were designed.

Once you have a complete understanding, you must seek to complete the assignment one step at a time, with God's guidance. Time is of the essence. Once we know what our assignment is, we cannot sit around twiddling our thumbs procrastinating because God's work is of the utmost importance. Psalm 90:12 says, *"So teach us to number our days, that we may apply our hearts unto wisdom."* It is imperative that we use our time wisely and not squander it on foolish things.

With God's guidance, you can complete all He has placed into your hands. So, soldiers, are you ready for the journey that lies ahead?

Chapter One
Getting an Understanding

"Wisdom is the principal thing; therefore get wisdom: and with all thy getting get understanding."
Proverbs 4:7

As Anastasia snuggled in her bed, pulling the sheets around her neck, she tried to shield her body from the cold breeze the air conditioner blew directly onto her. It was eleven o'clock at night, and no matter what she tried, she could not fall asleep. That had been her pattern for the past week and a half even though her normal bedtime was around ten o'clock.

Ever since she had attended Dr. C. White-Elliott's workshop titled "Time is Running Out," she could hear Dr. C.'s voice ringing in her ears, guiding her in identifying God's plan for her life. She desperately needed His guidance, during this new season in her life, and wanted to be obedient to His Word because the Bible says, *"Obedience is better than sacrifice"* (I Samuel 15:22). She recalled Dr. C. saying, "The book of Revelation says, 'Those who have an ear, let them hear what the spirit of the Lord is saying to the church'."

As a member of the body of Christ, Anastasia wanted to hear what the Lord had to say to her, so she could be instrumental in building God's kingdom and to ensure everything she did was by God's design and not her own. She had a deep desire to allow God to order her steps because the steps of a good man are ordered by the Lord (Psalm 37:23). She had no desire to lean to her own understanding, as she wanted to acknowledge God in all her ways (Proverbs 3:5-6).

Of everything Anastasia heard during the seminar, the most helpful was when Dr. C. included the six steps involved in learning, understanding, and fulfilling God's plan for one's life:

1. Building your faith,
2. Learning God's voice versus your own,
3. Understanding your assignment,
4. Receiving God's guidance,
5. Completing the task, and
6. Receiving the next step/assignment.

Before finally drifting off to sleep, after getting out of bed to turn off the air and to make a cup of chamomile tea, to relax her body and mind, Anastasia remembered the first bit of information Dr. C. shared with the attendees: *"I must work the works of him that sent me, while it is day: the night cometh, when no man can work"* (John 9:4).

During the night, Anastasia slept, but her sleep was interrupted by a dream of a building that had many rooms. As she traversed the hallways of the building, she felt as though she was in a maze. She had difficulty finding her way from one point to the next. Although each room was filled with peace, the journey of where to go next or exactly what she was to do in the building were the questions that were left unanswered.

The next morning, as Anastasia showered, dressed, and packed her briefcase, she pondered the meaning of the dream, but she knew the revelation would come in God's timing, as she could make no headway with it. After all, the Bible does say, *"For my thoughts are not your thoughts, neither are your ways my ways, saith the Lord. For as the heavens are higher than the earth, so are my ways higher than your ways, and my thoughts than your thoughts"* (Isaiah 55:8-9). With that understanding, Anastasia left well enough alone. After all, that was not Anastasia's first experience with have a confusing dream. One thing she had learned was everything is not always what it seems. Images usually signify something other than what they were in a dream. Colors are usually symbols of something too.

At one time, Anastasia had tried doing research, so she could have a better understanding of her dreams. She attended conferences and seminars where the speakers' topic was dreams. She listened intently and purchased their CDs and books. But, her efforts supplied very little information and few answers. Her quest to understand the symbolic meanings of her dreams led her nowhere fast. So, she had learned to wait for God for the revelations of any dreams she had. Sometimes, she had to wait for years for clear understanding.

Then, while getting into her car, she remembered the thought she had before she fell asleep, regarding the question Dr. C. had asked about John 9:4. She had asked for volunteers in the audience to explain what the verse meant. There were over 200 people in attendance at the seminar, and several lifted their hands to answer. But, to make the session manageable and in an attempt to not spend an inordinate amount of time, Dr. C. selected only three of the volunteers to provide their perspectives.

The first person, a pretentious looking man in his seventies, spoke loudly saying, "Each person has a responsibility to work. The Bible says a man who doesn't work doesn't eat. So, we each have a responsibility to fend for ourselves." The second person, an overzealous teenager with wired-framed glasses, was a brave soul to volunteer. She stated she really did not know the answer, but she wanted to take a stab at it. She said, "People must work during the day when the sun is out because at night it is hard to see." Speaking with assuredness, the third person said, "The words *day* and *night* refer to seasons, and there are seasons in our life when we are required to serve."

Dr. C. politely thanked the three volunteers for their responses; then, she took a poll of the audience to see which volunteer they believed was most likely correct: volunteer one, two, or three. Most of the audience agreed with the first and third volunteers. The audience was so certain of who was correct that they began to explain their reasoning to one another and even debate. Standing with a smile on her face, Dr. C. allowed the lively banter to continue for a few minutes.

After making the audience wait and allowing their curiosity to grow, Dr. C. explained her perspective on the verse. First, she said, "Volunteer number one's statement regarding the Bible stating if a man doesn't work, he doesn't eat is true; however, that is not what John 9:4 is referring to." The audience members who had selected volunteer one's answer were disappointed. Their sighs could be heard throughout the room.

Secondly, Dr. C. stated, "Volunteer number two wasn't too far off when she said a person can only work when he/she is able to see. But, there is more to it." Listening intently at that point, feeling they were getting closer to hearing the answer, the audience members quietly nodded their heads.

Thirdly, she stated, "Volunteer three mentioned seasons of work, meaning things change throughout the seasons of one's life. That statement is absolutely true because nothing stays the same. So, let's put volunteer two's statement and volunteer three's statement together to comprise the complete meaning. What John 9:4 is referring to is the season of life versus the season of death (or the afterlife). When John says a man must work while it is day, he is referring to the time we spend *alive* versus the time *after death*. We can only work while we are alive. Once we die, it is too late to do anything. Thus, we have the metaphors of *day* and *night*. The usage of the words *day* and *night* must not be taken literally. In comparing *day* to *night*, most people work during the daytime hours because it is difficult to accomplish many jobs in the dark. Darkness renders us ineffective."

Dr. C. continued her explanation with an example. "For example, construction workers do not typically work once dusk falls because it is too dark to see how to put the building together. They are much more effective and can work much faster in daylight hours to accomplish the desired goal. Therefore, a person must not squander his/her gift or ignore his/her assignment. We each have a responsebility to do what we have been gifted and called to do. And there is a limited amount of time for us to do it. Also, volunteer three mentioned seasons. The tasks God assigns to our hands may or may not be lifelong tasks. Some assignments last only a short time while others are lifelong. If a task only lasts for a portion of our life, we can be sure there was another task before it, and another one will come after it. We must always have the mindset of being about our Father's business (Luke 2:49). Furthermore, Psalm 90:12 says, *'So teach us to number our days, that we may apply our hearts unto wisdom.'* Tomorrow is not promised to any man; therefore, we must work while it is day.

After explaining the intended meaning of John 9:4, Dr. C. transitioned into another scripture that further explained the importance of not wasting time and to do what needs to be done at the proper moment.

> Proverbs says in 6:6-11, *"Go to the ant, you sluggard; consider its ways and be wise! It has no commander, no overseer or ruler, yet it stores its provisions in summer and gathers its food at harvest. How long will you lie there, you sluggard? When will you get up from your sleep? A little sleep, a little slumber, a little folding of the hands to rest— and poverty will come on you like a thief and scarcity like an armed man."*

This set of verses instructs men to follow the ant's example of being diligent about the tasks that need to be accomplished without a master or ruler commanding them to be done.

Basically, when we know what to do, we should just do it. Then, the verse continues, by providing the consequences if one should fail to obey: he/she will fall into poverty as a result of procrastinating or refusing to answer God's call. In reference to 'poverty' and 'obedience' to God's call, the meaning is as follows: when a person fails to obey God, he/she will not reap the benefits one would receive when he/she does what he/she is called to do. He/she may not experience poverty as it relates to money, but in one way or another, there will be lack.

Therefore, to avoid lack in one's life, a believer should become aware of his/her God-given assignment and make every attempt to fulfill it, thereby using the bestowed gifts and talents as intended.

Chapter Two
How Strong is Your Faith?

"So then faith cometh by hearing, and hearing by the word of God."
Romans 10:17

Sitting at the kitchen table, Anastasia removed the folder she had received at Dr. C's seminar from her briefcase. She had been carrying it around for a couple of weeks now. After meditating on Dr. C.'s words for the past few days, she thought it was time to review the steps, so she could put them into action. Step One in understanding God's plan for her life was to ensure she had the proper amount of faith to follow through with her assignment. According to Romans 10:17, a person's faith is developed by hearing the Word of God. And Anastasia had heard time and time again that some people had no faith, while others have little faith, and some had great faith.

Dr. C. had instructed the seminar participants to create a list of accomplishments/achievements in their life that they could only have possibly accomplished by stepping out on faith and to include the steps required to achieve the goal. On a blank sheet of paper, Anastasia formed the following list:

- began college at San Diego State University, with the intent to earn a Bachelor's degree in Liberal Studies (education emphasis). My desire was to teach elementary school, particularly third grade. To achieve that goal, I was required to move away from home, leaving my mother and brothers for the first time. I secured a job and an apartment only one week before I was scheduled to move. The entire process was daunting, but I made it through with my mother's assistance.

- completed the Bachelor's degree at Cal State University, Long Beach, after transferring from San Diego and taking classes each semester and supplemental classes each summer at the local community college. Some summers, I attended two community colleges: one in the daytime and the other in the evening. Each college had a limit on how many courses could be taken during the summer session. To fulfill my goal of graduating by a specific date, I had to take that alternate measure to meet my self-imposed goal.

- passed the CBEST (California Basic Educational Skills Test for educators) on the first attempt, after studying and taking practice exams. Passing the state-level test was a requirement that could not be circumvented if one wanted to teach in California's public school sector. To ensure I passed the exam, I practiced and practiced and practiced, every waking moment I had. Once the time came to take the exam, I was surprised to see how easy it was for me. The actual test was much easier than any of the practice exams.
That experience led me to organize and prepare other pre-service teachers for their next attempt at the CBEST, after they had taken the test and not passed one or more areas.

- obtained my first job with a school district to teach elementary school

- transitioned from elementary school to become a high school English teacher when a position became open and I was recommended for the position

- enrolled in the Master's program in English Composition at California State University, San Bernardino and finished the program, while working full time as a high school English teacher

- heard of an open position for a speech instructor at Crafton Hills College. I called the number I was given, which was to the department chair, and inquired about the position. I was asked to submit my resume. I promptly faxed it over, and I was hired over the phone for my very first job as a college professor.

- walked into the department chair's office at Chaffee College to apply for a job as an English professor rather than going to the Human Resources Department, which is proper protocol. Something in me said to talk to the person who would ultimately make the decision about hiring. HR is only the go-between between the applicant and the hiring authority. My choice to follow my instinct proved positive. After I was told there were no positions currently available, less than a week later, I received a call stating more classes opened up and an instructor was needed. I readily accepted the position.

- opened *A Step Above the Rest* tutorial service in the city of Rialto, without having to obtain a building, materials, or pay rent. I came in contact with a teacher who operated a charter school. He said he had heard about my wanting to open a tutorial service. I told him he was correct. He offered his school to me to use afterhours. He did not request any rent and permitted me to use his supplies. I had my own materials, so all I had to do was direct my students to his address, and the tutorial center came alive.

- purchased my first home with no money down. While teaching at an adult school, I came in contact with a Christian realtor. The thought of purchasing a home jumped into my spirit. I had never given it any thought before. Once I began speaking with the realtor, I could see the possibility of owning a home. I began to proclaim to my mother that I was going to purchase a home.

I began my search of properties, only to be disappointed in their condition. I never knew I was so germ conscious until I began to think about how I wanted to make a long-term investment. My realtor assured me that I would know the house when I saw it. Finally, she sent me to the High Desert, a place I had never heard of. I took the drive and fell in love with a house that was currently under construction. When I saw how white and spotless everything was, I knew I had found my home.

However, once my realtor contacted the contractor, we learned the property had been sold. But, there was good news to be given. The contractor said he had another home, the exact same model, on a street a few blocks over, and it was available. I took down the address and went to survey the property. My heart leaped. The next day, I sat at the table and listened to my realtor negotiate the deal. I signed the paper, hoping to become a home owner- that is if escrow cleared. For the next 30 days, I fasted and did everything I was instructed to do by the escrow company. Thirty days later, I moved into my brand new home that was free from germs!

- wrote and published my first book titled *Public Speaking in the Spiritual Arena.* After teaching speech classes at Crafton Hills College, I began to apply my teachings to the spiritual arena. Each time I sat in a worship service, I could see how God's people could benefit from the same principals experts applied when addressing audiences. So, shortly after, I began to hold seminars on public speaking. Then, a good friend recommended I take my training materials and compile it into a book. I followed his suggestion, and my first book was composed in one week.

- enrolled in the doctoral program in education at Capella University. I desired to take my education to the next level, so I surveyed different schools that offered graduate degrees. One day, I saw a commercial advertising Capella University and its degree programs. I decided to call. Subsequently, I liked what I heard when I spoke with an advisor, so I enrolled in classes and embarked upon a new journey.

- wrote and published five more books over the next several years while completing my doctoral studies

- founded a ministry: International Women's Commission with five other women by my side

- was licensed as a minister of the gospel of Jesus Christ. After speaking with my pastor about hearing God say "missionary" to me, I received a letter from my church stating I would be licensed for ministry at our next convocation. I was elated and re-read the letter several times as tears streamed down my face. I called everyone I knew and shared the news. I was truly honored to be a servant of God.

- completed the doctoral program, earning my PhD. After one year of taking classes and two years of writing my dissertation, I boarded a plan, heading to Minnesota. The headquarters for my school was based there, and I had to be physically present to participate in graduation. The ceremonies were spread over two days. It was the best graduation I had ever experienced, and it was done in style. On the plane ride home, I proudly wore my tam, as I grinned from ear to ear all the way back home.

- took my publishing company public by opening an office in Ontario, after publishing only my own books for six years along with those of a few other people

After composing her list in a matter of minutes, Anastasia had to take out a fresh sheet of paper because she realized the paper she had been writing on was covered with teardrops. That was the first time she had ever made a list of her accomplishments, and she was so proud and honored of how God had moved in her life. She had achieved so much, and all of her dreams had been fulfilled, with the exception of one. That particular dream required much more commitment and expense than any other dream she had ever attempted to achieve. And quite frankly, it made her a little nervous. She would definitely need to step out on faith to accomplish the God-given task that was set before her. However, she was determined to make her best attempts, with God's assistance and guidance.

Once her list was re-written, Anastasia reflected on each bullet point and had flashbacks of several younger versions of herself, reminiscing about past times and achievements. After an hour had passed, she concluded that she had successfully completed step one, after walking with the Lord for over 30 years and sitting under the preached Word, and being a preacher herself who diligently study the Word of God. That isn't to say that the unfulfilled assignment didn't take a higher measure of faith because it certainly did. And, Anastasia realized that. But she was also fully aware that Scripture says, *"Be strong and courageous. Do not be afraid or terrified because of them, for the LORD your God goes with you; he will never leave you nor forsake you"* (Deuteronomy 31:6). She was confident that God would order her steps and direct her paths, leading her to the desired destination He preordained for her.

Chapter Three
Whose Voice Is It?

The next week, after Sunday's worship service, Anastasia went home and made a bite to eat. After her meal, she reclined in her plush La-Z-Boy recliner with the folder labeled "Time is Running Out."

She was ready to examine her life to see if she had achieved *Step Two – Hearing God's Voice*. She was very familiar with the foundational verse Dr. C. had used that is repeated in several places in the book of Revelation: He who has an ear let him hear what the Spirit of the Lord is saying. Anastasia found herself constantly using those words in many of her own sermons.

But as Dr. C. had stated, the question, "How do I discern God's voice?" often arises. Believers know they should hear God's voice, but in different stages of their spiritual development, they may question whether or not they actually hear or recognize God's voice.

To assist the seminar attendees, Dr. C. provided eight verses for them to review and on which to meditate, so they would have a better understanding of how to hear God's voice. With the list in her hand, Anastasia began to review it. While reading, her eyes kept drifting from the page. Eventually, she fell asleep.

Anastasia was a chronic dreamer. At least five of seven nights per week, she dreamt several dreams per night. However, she did not always remember her dreams when she awoke. Moreover, for the dreams she could recall, she didn't always remember the complete dream. Turning on her side, Anastasia snuggled her head deeper into the headrest of the recliner, making herself more comfortable. The dream she had the week before replayed again, except that time she felt more secure and felt she had a sense of direction. The building was still empty, but Anastasia felt a sense of belonging. She felt as though she was meant to be there even though she didn't know the purpose.

An hour later, Anastasia stirred in the chair, not realizing she had fallen asleep. Slowly, she rose to her feet, causing the list to fall to the floor. After retrieving it, she began to go through the list of verses again, as she retook her seat.

Proverbs 3:5-6: *Trust in the Lord with all thine heart; and lean not unto thine own understanding. In all thy ways acknowledge him, and he shall direct thy paths.*

Trust in the Lord with all thine heart, not in a creature, the best, the holiest, and the highest; not in any creature enjoyment, as riches, strength, and wisdom; nor in any outward privilege, arising from natural descent and education; not in a man's self, in his own heart, which is deceitful; nor in any works of righteousness done by him; not in a profession of religion, or the duties of it, ever so well performed; not in frames, nor in graces, and the exercise of them; no, not in faith or trust itself: but in the Lord, the object of all grace, and in him only; in Jehovah the Father, as the God of nature and providence, for all temporal blessings; and as the God of all grace, for all spiritual blessings, and all the needful supplies of grace; and for eternal happiness, which he has provided, promised, and freely gives.

Trust in Him at all times; in times of affliction, temptation, and darkness: there is a great deal of reason for it; all power and strength are in him to help; his love, grace, and mercy, move him to it, and are always the same: the consideration of what he has done for others that have trusted in him, and for ourselves in times past, should induce and encourage to it; as also the happiness of those that trust in him, who enjoy peace and safety; and his displeasure at those that show any diffidence of him, or distrust him.

Trust in God the Son; in His person for acceptance; in His righteousness for justification; in His blood for pardon; in His fulness for supply; in His power for protection and preservation; and in Him alone for salvation and eternal life. Trust in Jehovah the Spirit, to carry on and finish the work of grace upon the heart; of which a saint may be confident that where it is begun it will be completed. And this trust in Father, Son, and Spirit, should be "with all the heart," cordial and sincere.

The phrase denotes not so much the strength of faith as the sincerity of it; it signifies a faith unfeigned; it is not saying, or professing, that a man believes and trusts in the Lord; but it is with the heart, and with his whole heart, that he believes unto righteousness, if he believes aright; see Romans 10:10; and lean not unto thine own understanding; or trust not to that; for it stands opposed to trusting in the Lord.

Men should not depend upon their own wisdom and understanding, in the conduct of civil life, but should seek the direction and blessing of Providence, or otherwise will meet with disappointment; and, when they succeed, should ascribe it not to their own prudence and wisdom, but to the goodness of God; for "bread" is not always "to the wise, nor riches to men of understanding," Ecclesiastes 9:11; and much less should men lean to their own understanding in matters of religion; a natural man has no understanding of spiritual things, of the things of the Gospel, nor indeed any practical understanding of things moral, Romans 3:11, Jeremiah 4:22.

The understanding of man is darkened by sin; yea, is darkness itself; it is like the first earth, covered with darkness, till light is let into it, and therefore not to be leaned unto and depended on, Ephesians 4:18. There is a necessity of a new heart and spirit, of an understanding to be given, in order to understand spiritual and divine things, Ezekiel 36:26; for though these are not contrary to the reason and understanding of men; yet they are above them, and cannot be discovered, reached, comprehended, and accounted for by them, Matthew 16:17.

Nay, there are some things in the Gospel, which, though plain to an enlightened understanding by the word of God, yet the manner how they are cannot be apprehended: as the doctrines of a trinity of Persons; of the generation of the Son of God; the procession of the Spirit; the union of the two natures in Christ; the resurrection of the dead, &c. In short, not our reason and understanding at best, and much less as carnal and unsanctified, but the word of God only is our rule of judgment, and the standard of our faith and practice; and to that we should have recourse and be directed by it, and not lean to our own understandings (John Gill's Exposition of the Bible).

Proverbs 11:14: *Where no counsel is, the people fall: but in the multitude of counsellors there is safety.*

A good leader needs and uses wise advisers. One person's perspective and understanding is severely limited; he/she may not have all the facts or may be blinded by bias, emotions, or wrong impressions. To be a wise leader at home, at church, or at work, seek the counsel of others and be open to their advice. Then, after considering all the facts, make your decision.

A person qualifies as godly counsel when he/she has a strong relationship with God and a good understanding of His Word. This is demonstrated by possessing a moral character and integrity. This person will not deviate from God's Word and will speak His oracles.

Isaiah 30:21: *And thine ears shall hear a word behind thee, saying, This is the way, walk ye in it, when ye turn to the right hand, and when ye turn to the left.*

When the people of Jerusalem left God's path, He would correct them. He will do the same for us, as He is no respecter of persons. However, when we hear His voice of correction, we must be willing to follow it!

The more we tune our ears to hear from God, especially when we are being corrected, the more He will speak to us.

Jeremiah 29:12-13: *Then shall ye call upon me, and ye shall go and pray unto me, and I will hearken unto you. And ye shall seek me, and find me, when ye shall search for me with all your heart.*

In times of dire circumstances, it may appear as though God has forgotten you. But God may be preparing you, as He did the people of Judah, for a new beginning with Him at the center. According to God's wise plan, His people were to have a future and a hope. Consequently, they could call upon Him in confidence. If we seek Him wholeheartedly, He will be found. Neither a strange land, sorrow, persecution, nor physical problem can break our fellowship with God.

We should seek God's guidance every day of our lives. We should call upon His name. When we make this a regular practice, we will begin to recognize His voice when He answers.

John 10:4-5: *And when he putteth forth his own sheep, he goeth before them, and the sheep follow him: for they know his voice. And a stranger will they not follow, but will flee from him: for they know not the voice of strangers.*

The body of Christ is a sheepfold and is exposed to deceivers and persecutors. The great Shepherd of the sheep knows all that are His, guards them by His providence, guides them by His Spirit and Word, and goes before them, to set them in the way of His steps. The spirit of Christ will set before them an open door. The sheep of Christ will observe their shepherd and be cautious and shy of strangers, who would draw them from faith in Him to fantasies about him.

Once a person commits his/her life to Christ, a bond is forged and the person is not easily swayed by another's voice or actions. Therefore, it is imperative that we build a solid relationship with Chrit.

I Thessalonians 5:19-21: *Quench not the Spirit. Despise not prophesyings. Prove all things; hold fast that which is good.*

By warning us not to stifle the Holy Spirit, Apostle Paul means that we should not ignore or toss aside the gifts the Holy Spirit gives. Here, he mentions prophecy. Sometimes, spiritual gifts are controversial, and they may cause division in the church. Rather than trying to solve the problems, some Christians prefer to smother the gifts. This impoverishes the church. We should not stifle the Holy Spirit's work in anyone's life but encourage the full expression of these gifts to benefit the whole body of Christ.

Prophecy has been and still is a way that God speaks to His people. However, we should test the words that are spoken against words in the Bible. There should be no contradiction.

II Timothy 3:16-17: *All scripture is given by inspiration of God, and is profitable for doctrine, for reproof, for correction, for instruction in righteousness: That the man of God may be perfect, thoroughly furnished unto all good works.*

The entire Bible is God's inspired Word. Because it is inspired and trustworthy, we should read it and apply it to our life. We never have to wonder when we are reading God's Word whether or not He is speaking to us, as the Bible is His voice.

-is profitable for doctrine;

for the discovering, illustrating, and confirming any doctrine concerning God, the being, persons, and perfections of God; concerning the creation and fall of man; concerning the person and offices of Christ, redemption by him, justification by his righteousness, pardon by his blood, reconciliation and atonement by his sacrifice, and eternal life through him, with many others. The Scripture is profitable for ministers to fetch doctrine from, and establish it by; and for hearers to try and prove it by:

-for reproof;

of errors and heresies; this is the sword of the Spirit, which cuts all down. There never was, nor is, nor can be any error or heresy broached in the world, but there is a sufficient refutation of it in the Scriptures; which may be profitably used for that purpose, as it often has been by Christ and his apostles, and others since in all ages:

-for correction; of vice; there being no sin, but the evil nature of it is shown, its wicked tendency is exposed, and the sad effects and consequences of it are pointed out in these writings: for instruction in righteousness; in every branch of duty incumbent upon men; whether with respect to God, or one another; for there is no duty men are obliged unto, but the nature, use, and excellency of it, are here shown: the Scriptures are a perfect rule of faith and practice; and thus they are commended from the usefulness and profitableness of them (John Gill's Exposition of the Bible).

Hebrews 5:14: *But strong meat belongeth to them that are of full age, even those who by reason of use have their senses exercised to discern both good and evil.*

But strong meat belongeth to them that are of full age, or perfect; see 1 Corinthians 2:6. This does not intend a perfection of justification; for though some have a greater degree of faith than others, and a clearer discovery of their justification, yet babes in Christ are as perfectly justified as more grown and experienced believers; nor a perfection of sanctification, for there is no perfection of holiness but in Christ; and though the work of sanctification may be in greater perfection in one saint than in another, yet all are imperfect in this life; and as to a perfection of parts, babes have this as well as adult persons: but it designs a perfection of knowledge; for though none are entirely perfect, yet some have arrived to a greater degree of the knowledge of Gospel mysteries than others, and to these the strong meat of the Gospel belongs; they are capable of understanding the more mysterious parts of the Gospel; of searching into the deep things of God; and of receiving and digesting the more sublime truths of the Christian religion: even those who by reason of use, have their senses exercised to discern both good and evil; that is, their spiritual senses, the internal senses of the understanding and judgment, signified by external ones; as by seeing the Son; hearing the voice of Christ; savoring or smelling a sweet odor in the things of God, and Christ; tasting that the Lord is gracious; feeling and handling the word of life, as these are held forth in the everlasting

Gospel: and these being exercised on their proper object, by use, an habit is contracted; and such are qualified for discerning, as between moral good and evil, and the worse and better state of the church, and between law and Gospel, so between the doctrines of Christ, and the doctrines of men; who find they differ: the doctrines of Christ such experienced persons find to be good, wholesome, nourishing, and salutary; and the doctrines of men to be evil, to eat, as does a canker, and to be pernicious, poisonous, and damnable; and the discernment they make, and the judgment they form, are not according to the dictates of carnal reason, but according to the Scriptures of truth, and their own experience (John Gill's Exposition of the Bible).

After reading the eight sets of verses and their detailed commentary, Anastasia ascertained that hearing God's voice and recognizing it is predicated upon one's motive. When a person's heart is set on fulfilling his/her own desires, his/her focus will be on him/herself and not on God's will. On the other hand, when a person has surrendered his/her life to God and His will, he/she will have an open heart and ears to receive instructions from God. He/she will be waiting for opportunities to be used.

Anastasia sat down again in the recliner and reminisced on her walk with the Lord, recalling many instances where she had heard God's voice or He had done something unique to capture her attention. As she reflected, she was amazed at the amount of detail she recalled for each incident and how God's hand had been upon her life for a very, very long time. Tears of joy ran down her face as four specific instances came to her remembrance.

First, she recalled an experience that had only occurred once in her life: approximately twelve or thirteen years prior. She was in a hotel room asleep. She had taught a class that was a far distance from her home, so she had opted to spend the night near the location of the class and drive home the next morning. She had gone to bed at a decent time, but around 4-4:30 AM, she heard a doorbell ring. She slowly lifted her head from the pillow, attempting to get her bearings. She wondered who was at her front door. A few seconds later, she opened her eyes and saw the hotel room in the darkness. Understanding there was no one at the door because the rooms did not have doorbells, she laid her head back onto the pillow, without even bothering to check. Just as quickly as she laid her head down, she turned to her side and began to pray.

She had prior experiences with hearing a doorbell ring ever so often over the course of a year or two. She would get up in the wee hours of the morning, after hearing the doorbell, and walk to her front door to see who it could possibly be. Each time, to her surprise, there was no one there, but she was sure she had heard a single ring of her doorbell. Finally, she chalked it up to being part of a dream. After that occurred a few times, she realized the 'doorbell sound' was not a dream at all. It was the Lord trying to get her attention because He needed her to pray. That realization is what caused her to turn to her side to pray that morning in the hotel room.

After praying for only a short while, Anastasia soon fell asleep. Soon after, she began to dream, but it was no ordinary dream. It was a nightmare- to put it in mild terms! She dreamed she was at a church function that was sponsored by her church. The event wasn't in the church building; instead, it appeared to be in an arena. She saw many familiar faces of members who attended her church. Her pastor was even standing on the platform preaching. Everyone was excited about he was saying. As Anastasia praised God along with everyone else, a woman who was standing in front of her also praising the Lord turned around and faced her. When the woman turned around, her face transformed from a normal human face to the face of someone who was demon possessed. Horrified, Anastasia turned around to prevent looking at the demon that was bold enough to make direct eye contact with her. To her chagrin, when she turned around, her eyes landed on three individuals who were seated on a couch, and one of their faces transformed just like the first woman.

Immediately, Anastasia jarred herself awake and jumped up from the bed. She got down on the floor, with her knees bent, and began a prayer of repentance. She was repenting for disobeying God's request to pray. She had attempted, but she didn't really know what or who to pray for, so she had ended up falling asleep. While she was on the floor praying, the most awesome experience she ever had in her entire life occurred. The Shekinah glory of the Lord filled the room, but Anastasia would not open her eyes to witness it. She knew the presence of the Lord surrounded her. His glory was so bright that the room was completely lighted and warm. Remember, at 4 AM, the room was still relatively dark, but the light was so bright, Anastasia could see it through closed eyelids.

Continuing to pray, not wanting to see anymore evil faces, Anastasia kept her face to the floor. Then, she felt the presence of someone standing in front of her. Lifting her head, she saw a man who glowed brightly holding a scepter. In reverence, Anastasia bowed her head again. The man lifted the scepter and placed it on her right shoulder and then her left shoulder. Understanding she had just been anointed for the Lord's service, Anastasia began to weep, feeling honored that the Lord Himself had chosen her.

Not much later after that experience, International Women's Commission, which had already been in the process of being formed, had its first conference one month later. There were over one hundred people in attendance. The ministry was designed to focus on the complete person: spiritual, educational, financial, emotional, and sexual with an emphasis on healing and deliverance; hence, the dreams about demons.

The *second* event Anastasia recalled was being in attendance at the closing service of a weeklong conference at her church. It was during the late afternoon on a Sunday, and she was seated in the pulpit, along with other ministers and pastors. The words the guest minister spoke were so powerful that Anastasia jumped up from her seat, praising God while still listening intently to the next words the preacher would say. As she stood there listening to his proclamations, a vision of a sign flashed before her eyes. Before she knew it, she was turning around in a circle in the tight row of the pulpit. Then, she sat down as the tears fell from her eyes.

Three days before, on a Thursday, Anastasia had parked her car and began walking toward a university for which she taught classes. Just before she passed through the front doors, she saw a "for lease" sign sitting on the ground leaning against the building. The sign caught her attention because it was in an odd position, but other than that she didn't pay close attention to it.

Sitting on the seat in the pulpit with the vision of the sign still in her mind, Anastasia knew exactly what the Lord was saying to her. Earlier that week, Anastasia had had fleeting thoughts of opening an office for her publishing company: CLF Publishing. She did not know why or how the desire had become so strong. She had never given it a thought before. At that time, the publishing company was a home-based business, and Anastasia was content with that. She never looked to publish full-time, as she was content with her teaching profession. But she knew in her heart that the vision of the sign was God telling her to step out on faith and take her company public.

On her drive home, Anastasia was very excited, so much so she found it hard to sleep that night. She dreamt of offices all night with a sense of excitement of her new adventure.

Being obedient, the next morning, Anastasia walked out of her bedroom and across the hall into her home office and immediately began searching the web for office spaces for lease. In the midst of searching online, her cell phone rang. On the other end was a leasing agent offering her to come and view offices the next day. Anastasia was completely confused as to how he received her phone number and was even more amazed when he stated he was calling from a company that had offices in a building located on the same street as the university, where she had seen the "for lease" sign. She accepted the agent's invitation to come in. However, she had already had two other appointments scheduled prior to that one.

The next day, she went to view two office spaces and was pleased with what she saw. However, the requested lease amounts were exorbitant. Although that was a little discouraging, Anastasia pressed forward and tried to stay positive because in the back of her mind, she knew God would not send her own a wild goose chase. It was just a matter of finding the right office, at the right price, to fit her needs. Finally, it was time to go to the last appointment- the mystery phone call she had received the day before.

She was ready and had her game face on. The agent was very professional and greeted her with a smile. After a few minutes of discussion, she was given the lease price. She respectfully declined stating the price was out of her range. Prior to going to view office spaces, Anastasia had gone over her budget, and she knew what was affordable for her. Furthermore, she knew the Bible warned against being anxious. So, she would not allow herself to move toward gaining an office space without using wisdom simply because she liked what she saw.

When Anastasia gathered her purse to leave, the agent quickly stopped her and asked her to name her price, stating the floor of that office building was being renovated and would be designed into eighty different offices, and he had permission to allow the first ten lessees to name their price- within reason. Anastasia decided to test him for truthfulness and named a price. She wasn't sure which direction the conversation would go and what the outcome would be, but she decided to give it a shot. After all, what did she have to lose? She had taken the time to drive the distance to the location, so a few more minutes could not hurt.

After stating an amount she would be comfortable paying (half the amount the agent had originally stated), to her extreme surprise, he accepted, and she signed the papers. A few months later, renovations were completed, and she moved in. Within one month, Anastasia had ten new publishing clients- all because she stepped out on faith!

The *third* event Anastasia recalled also had transpired in church. One bright and beautiful Sunday morning, Anastasia stood in the sanctuary of her church. She had just finished teaching Sunday school and had begun to survey the auditorium to see who was inside. As her eyes came across one of the female members, the Holy Spirit sparked something in her, giving her instructions.

Upon hearing the instructions, Anastasia hesitated, as she was surprised at what the Lord had said. He had instructed her to go over to the woman and give words of encouragement. What caused Anastasia's hesitation was the woman's history in the church as it related to speaking with other members. She had a standoffish attitude and did not take being approached very well. Anastasia and the woman had never greeted each other, let alone had any words at all. Anastasia did not know how the woman would receive being approached, so she hesitated a moment longer as she continued to speak to another member. When she heard the words of the Lord again, she excused herself from the member she was speaking with and made her way to the woman.

As Anastasia walked down the center aisle between the pews, the walk seemed longer than usual. But Anastasia stayed focused and kept her eyes on the goal. The woman saw her approaching and did not return a friendly smile when Anastasia smiled at her.

Nevertheless, Anastasia was on a mission, determined to be obedient to the Lord's instructions. When she reached the woman, she said to her the exact words the Lord had given her. The woman received the words Anastasia offered but without a smile. The look the woman had on her face showed Anastasia she did not believe what she had said although the words were positive and the woman has said, "Thank you." God had not told Anastasia to offer an explanation, so Anastasia, having completed her task, turned around to leave.

That God-given assignment was unlike any other assignments God had given to Anastasia. Most assignments were ones she readily agreed to. That assignment, however, made her uncomfortable, but she is always careful to remember that the Bible says obedience is better than sacrifice (I Samuel 15:22). Moreover, the rewards of being obedient are greater than she could ever imagine.

The *fourth* event Anastasia recalled still amazes her today although it doesn't measure in comparison to the experience with the Shekinah glory. One day, after giving it some thought over the past several months, Anastasia decided it was time for her to purchase a new car. However, she knew it would be best to take her time to find the right vehicle. And she was confident the Lord would guide her in the right direction, if she sought His guidance.

Anastasia began her car search by going online and surveying several cars that were available at different car dealerships. Her search led her to go and view the vehicles in person, to get an idea of their true condition and sticker price. In her quest, she visited two dealerships. The first dealership was one she had never heard of before but was delighted to visit because the cars they had disbursed about the parking lot were simply beautiful. While at the dealership, she took the salesperson's advice and filled out an application to see what the qualification criteria would be. Displeased with what she heard, Anastasia promptly left the dealership in a sour mood. Then she made her way down the street to the second dealership with which she was familiar because she had purchased her current vehicle there.

She was familiar with their terms of purchase, so she proceeded to look around the lot. One vehicle in the corner of the front of the lot caught her eye immediately. She inquired with the salesperson who was in the parking lot about the down payment for the vehicle. As she suspected, the down payment request was extremely high. Disappointedly, Anastasia returned to her vehicle, started the car, and pulled out of the parking lot.

On one hand, she was disappointed, but on the other hand, she was not discouraged. She knew she was only in the beginning stages of purchasing a vehicle and knew that eventually she would. If it meant saving up for the down payment, that is what she was determined to do. Given the numbers Anastasia had heard that day for the required deposit for the type of vehicle she desired to purchase, she quickly devised a plan to save the down payment.

Over the course of the following two months, Anastasia went about her normal routine, and each time she received a paycheck, she placed money aside. During that time, one of the vehicles never left her mind. She could see herself driving it, and her desire began to grow. Every other week or so, Anastasia would go back online to the dealership's website to see if the car was still available. Each time she checked, the car was still there. One time though, Anastasia was surprised by what she saw. The dealership had dropped the price on the car several thousand dollars. That made Anastasia more determined than ever to reach her goal of saving the down payment, and she had a feeling that the car was meant to be hers.

However, Anastasia was more determined not to go before the Lord said it was time to move. And no matter how much she had a fancy for that the particular car, she would not claim that the car was hers because she had not heard the Lord say so. For all she knew, God had something else in store for her. Therefore, she continued to save her money and keep her ears open for any direction God would give her.

One day, Anastasia received a phone call from one of her brothers, requesting a loan. She told him she could loan him the money, but she needed it back on a particular day because she was going to purchase a car on May 5. He told her he would return the money on May 1. When Anastasia disconnected the call, she wondered why she had told her brother she was going to purchase a car on May 5 because she had not reached her down payment goal nor had the Lord told her to move.

A couple of weeks later, early in the morning on a Saturday, the Lord told Anastasia to return to the car dealership where she had seen the car that really moved her. Sitting on her bed, Anastasia knew she had heard the voice of the Lord clearly, but she was utterly confused. Her day was filled with appointments, and she did not have all of the money the salesperson had said she would need to purchase the car. Nevertheless, Anastasia believed the Lord. As she prepared for her day, she wondered if she should cancel one of her appointments in order to go to the dealership, as the Lord had instructed. Each appointment was extremely important and involved other people. Anastasia is a woman of her word and did not want to cancel any of her appointments. She just had to believe that the Lord would make a way for her to go to the dealership.

After Anastasia completed her first two appointments, she once again got onto the freeway to make her way to the third and final appointment of the day. When she arrived to the location where she was to do a taping of her online TV show, she was surprised that another event was taking place and there was no set time for the event to end. At that point, Anastasia had a decision to make. She could wait it out and have her guests standby, or she could reschedule for another time. After some deliberation, Anastasia decided it would be best for all parties involved to reschedule the taping.

Once the taping had been postponed, Anastasia realized the rest of her afternoon was suddenly free. She checked her watch and saw that it was 3:30 in the afternoon, and her mind went directly to the dealership. The dealership would be open for another few hours.

Anastasia got back in her car and returned to the freeway, making her way to the dealership. She was disappointed that she was unable to tape her show, but she was more in awe of how God had opened a path for her to do what He had told her to do earlier that morning before she arose, without having to purposefully break her commitments.

Driving to the dealership, Anastasia wondered what would happen when she got there. She did not know if the car was still available since the last time she had checked the website and the salesperson had been very clear about what amount they wanted for the down payment. Her brother had paid back the loan just two days before, but she still did not have the required amount. She knew her journey was a journey of faith.

As Anastasia turned into the driveway of the dealership, she could see that the car she had her eyes on was still there, parked in the same spot that it had been when she had seen it a couple of months before. As she walked over to the car with a smile on her face, a familiar salesperson approached her. She stated to him that the car was still there since the last time she had visited the lot and that meant the car was hers. He asked her to come inside to discuss it. Confidently, she followed him into one of the dealership's offices.

Allow me to clarify her level of confidence. Anastasia was confident that the car was meant to be hers; however, she was not confident about what the salesperson would say about the down payment.

As Anastasia sat at the salesperson's desk, the salesperson gave her the same figure that was given to her before on the amount they required as a down payment, even though the sticker price had been reduced. Calmly, Anastasia told him she did not have the required amount. He looked at her and asked, "How much do you have?" Anastasia gave him an amount, which was $3,000 less than the requested amount, and he replied, "Okay." The room fell silent, and no other words were spoken. To say the least, Anastasia was dumbfounded. She did not say a word.

The salesperson looked back to her and said, "Do you want to take the car today?" Anastasia could not believe what her ears were hearing, but she kept calm and simply replied, "I do not have the money with me today. It is at home. Are you guys open tomorrow?"

"No," the sales person said. "We are closed on Sundays."

"Okay," Anastasia replied. "I will need to bring it back on Monday." The salesperson agreed without hesitation.

On Monday, Anastasia returned to the dealership to pay the down payment and take possession of the vehicle. As she pulled out of the lot and onto the street, driving her new car, she was amazed at how God had moved and reflected on how the date was May 5 as she had proclaimed.

After examining her life and recalling the four events, Anastasia felt confident that she was a willing vessel to be used as the Lord saw fit. Therefore, her ears were open to hear from God. Were there areas she could improve upon? Of course there were. During her self-examination, Anastasia admitted that to herself as well. After her self-discovery, with a smile on her face, she placed a check in the box next to Step Two on the checklist Dr. C. had provided.

Chapter Four
Uniquely Designed

"Before I formed thee in the belly I knew thee; and before thou camest forth out of the womb I sanctified thee, and I ordained thee a prophet unto the nations" (Jeremiah 1:5). These are the words the Lord spoke to the prophet Jeremiah. Just as God designed Jeremiah to be a profit to the nations, He designed each and every person for a specific assignment to be fulfilled in the earth. God has need of all of us, and no one person is more important than another. I Corinthians 12:12 says, *"For as the body is one, and hath many members, and all the members of that one body, being many, are one body: so also is Christ."* In order for us to fulfill our assignment, we must be clear about what it is.

Those words were printed on the top of Dr. C's handout that provided the details of *Step Three: Understanding Your Assignment*. Included on the handout were five steps, and each were covered in detail. Dr. C. asked the attendees to read each step and fill in an example from their own life for each one, to assist in identifying and/or clarifying their assignment. When she asked how many people knew what their assignment was, the majority of the attendees raised their hands, while the minority had a slight idea or no clue whatsoever. At the end of the seminar, Dr. C. asked everyone to complete the worksheet even if they felt they were completely sure about their calling. Once the assignment was completed, each person would submit his/her responses electronically, so Dr. C. and her team could provide feedback.

To guide them, Dr. C. included several biblical examples to demonstrate God's plan for His people.

1. Moses

God created Moses for one specific assignment on earth: to bring out the children of Israel from Egypt.

Ex 3:10: *Come now therefore, and I will send you unto Pharaoh, that you may bring forth my people the children of Israel out of Egypt.*

Moses was forty years old when God spoke to him on Mt. Horeb. At that time, Moses was a sheep herder for his father-in-law Jethro. God gained Moses' attention when He set fire to a bush but did not allow the bush to be consumed by the fire. Once God had Moses' attention, He was able to give Moses an assignment – to return to Egypt with a message for Pharaoh – to permit the Israelites to leave Egypt. Moses did not feel equipped to deliver the message to Pharaoh. He complained about not being able to speak properly or having the proper authority to go before Pharaoh. Once God assured Moses that He would be with him, Moses took on the task and walked in obedience. Furthermore, there was a hedge of protection around Moses because God had anointed him. Moses was protected when he was born, when all Hebrew baby boys were being slain. He was also protected when he killed an Egyptian in the land of Egypt, during the time he lived in Pharaoh's home.

When Moses accomplished his assignment on earth, God gave him rest in His kingdom.

2. Joshua

God created Joshua for one specific assignment on earth: to lead the children of Israel across river Jordan into the Promised Land. Joshua was the man created by God to take over after Moses.

Joshua 1:1-2: *Now after the death of Moses the servant of the LORD it came to pass, that the LORD spoke unto Joshua the son of Nun, Moses' minister, saying, 'Moses my servant is dead; now therefore arise, go over this Jordan, you, and all this people, unto the land which I do give to them, even to the children of Israel'.*

After Moses died, it was natural for the person who was second in command to take the helm: Joshua. Moses had led the Israelites out of Egypt and into the wilderness, but they had not made it to the land that God had promised them: Canaan, the land flowing with milk and honey. Therefore, it was then Joshua's responsibility to get them there, but there was another obstacle they had to conquer: the river Jordan. With God guiding Joshua in leading the Israelites, there was no way he could fail. So, Joshua took up the mantle and marched forward, confident that God would not leave or forsake him.

3. David

God created David to shepherd and be a warrior for the children of Israel.

2 Samuel 7:8: *Now therefore so shall you say unto my servant David, Thus says the LORD of hosts, 'I took you from the sheepfold, from following the sheep, to be ruler over my people, over Israel'*

1 King 2:11: *And the days that David reigned over Israel were forty years: seven years reigned he in Hebron, and thirty and three years reigned he in Jerusalem.*

The Israelites asked God for a king, and God appointed Saul although He is the King of kings and Lord of lords, who is omnipotent. But Israel was stubborn, and they failed to realize God's sovereignty. However, when God commanded King Saul to attack the Amalekites and to spare no one, by killing all the people and animals, Saul did indeed attack the Amalekites, but he spared Agag, the king, and the best animals. God is not a god of compromise. He means what He says and wants nothing less.

Due to Saul's obedience, God removed him from his throne, naming David as Israel's second king. David accepted God's appointment to shepherd over the sheep, the Israelites.

4. Solomon

Solomon was created and placed on this earth to build the temple.

2 Samuel 7:12-13: *And when your days be fulfilled, and you sleep with your fathers, I will set up your seed after you, which shall proceed out of your bowels, and I will establish his kingdom. He shall build a house for my name, and I will establish the throne of his kingdom forever.*

1 King 6:14: *So Solomon built the temple, and finished it.*

David, Solomon's father, king of Israel, loved the Lord with all his heart and desired to build God a temple. God, however, denied David's request, saying David had blood on his hands. David was responsible for the death of Bathsheba's husband, Uriah the Hittite. David had Uriah killed during battle to cover up his sin: getting Bathsheba pregnant. Therefore, he was not suitable to build a home for the Lord. God further stated that David's son, Solomon, would be appointed for the task.

Four years after Solomon was appointed king, he began to build a temple for God. Seven years later, the temple was completed.

5. Jeremiah

Jeremiah was created and placed on earth to be a prophet.

Jeremiah 1:5: *Before I formed thee in the belly I knew you; and before you came forth out of the womb I sanctified you, and I ordained you a prophet unto the nations.*

When Jeremiah was called by God to be a prophet to the nation of Judah, Jeremiah responded by saying he was too young to speak and he did not know how. God rebuked him, telling him not to say he was too young. Man's viewpoint is often not the viewpoint God has. Our thoughts differ from God's thoughts and our ways are not His ways. God assured Jeremiah that he had nothing to worry about because He would be with Jeremiah every step of the way. All Jeremiah had to do was speak the words the Lord gave him to speak.

Jeremiah was obedient but expressed sadness throughout his ministry from all the disobedience to God he witnessed. Today, Jeremiah is known to Bible scholars and theologians as the weeping prophet.

6. Jonah

Jonah was created to take the repentance message to Nineveh.

Jonah 1:1-2: *Now the word of the LORD came unto Jonah the son of Amittai, saying, 'Arise, go to Nineveh, that great city, and cry against it; for their wickedness is come up before me'.*
Because of Jonah taking God's message to Nineveh, Nineveh repented and God relented from the disaster that He was to bring upon Nineveh.

Jonah 3:10: *And God saw their works, that they turned from their evil way; and God repented of the evil, that he had said that he would do unto them; and he did it not.*

Jonah, a prophet of God, was given the assignment of delivering a message to the Ninevites, so they would have an opportunity to repent before the Lord of all their evildoings. Jonah believed the Ninevites deserved to perish and, therefore, he refused to go and deliver the message. So, God had to deal with him and interrupt his escape by having him tossed overboard from a ship, landing him in the belly of a large fish. Jonah stayed there three days. Afterward, the fish expelled him, and Jonah finally came to his senses and obeyed the Lord.

7. John the Baptist

John the Baptist was created for only one assignment on earth: to be a voice in the wilderness preparing the way for Jesus.

Mt 3:1-2: *In those days came John the Baptist, preaching in the wilderness of Judaea, And saying, 'Repent: for the kingdom of heaven is at hand'.*

Isa 40:3: *The voice of him that cries in the wilderness, Prepare the way of the LORD, make straight in the desert a highway for our God.*

Mt 3:3: *For this is he that was spoken of by the prophet Isaiah, saying, 'The voice of one crying in the wilderness, Prepare the way of the Lord, make his paths straight'.*

A voice crying in the wilderness was prophesied by Isaiah many years ago before John the Baptist was created. From his creation by God even before his birth, John was ordained to be the voice.

The world had to be prepared for the coming of the Jewish Messiah, the Savior of the world, so a forerunner was created, as prophesied in the book of Isaiah. John the Baptist was the forerunner for Christ. He proclaimed Christ's coming and what He would do. When Christ arrived at the Jordan River to be baptized, John announced Jesus as the Lamb of God who would take away the sins of the world.

8. Paul

Paul was created to take the gospel to Gentiles.

Acts 9:15: *But the Lord said unto him, 'Go your way: for he is a chosen vessel unto me, to bear my name before the Gentiles, and kings, and the children of Israel'*

Acts 13:46-47: *Then Paul and Barnabas waxed bold, and said, 'It was necessary that the word of God should first have been spoken to you: but seeing you put it from you, and judge yourselves unworthy of everlasting life, lo, we turn to the Gentiles. For so has the Lord commanded us, saying, 'I have set you to be a light of the Gentiles, that you should be for salvation unto the ends of the earth'.*

Paul, born Saul of Tarsus, was notorious for persecuting followers of the Way (Christians- followers of Christ). In the midst of his plight to continue to persecute believers, Saul was on his way to Damascus. Suddenly, he was blinded by a bright light that shone down from heaven. In an instant, he was speaking to the Lord, and his course was changed from persecutor to agent of Christ. He was then on a mission to spread the gospel of Christ to Gentiles.

All of these people in the Bible accomplished their assignments on earth, and God gave them rest in His kingdom.

~~~~~~~~~

Instead of Anastasia sitting in her La-Z-Boy recliner and going back down memory lane in her mind to come up with examples for each step of the process, she decided to call a friend who had also gone to the seminar to see if she wanted to get together to complete their respective worksheets through oral conversation. When Janice answered the phone, she was in the middle of cooking dinner, but she was happy to hear from Anastasia. They had not seen each other since they had ridden together to the seminar. They did not live in the same city, so they actually only got together when they planned to.

Janice immediately accepted Anastasia's offer and sweetened the pot by inviting Anastasia over for dinner. Anastasia hadn't given much thought to what she was going to eat that evening, so a dinner invitation was right on time. Anastasia quickly picked up her briefcase and tossed the folder inside, as she made her way to her car.

Once Anastasia arrived to Janice's home, she greeted her friend and walked in to the welcoming smell of oregano, tomato sauce, onions, garlic, and all the other ingredients Janice included in her spaghetti sauce. Anastasia was always excited to eat Janice's cooking because she typically made everything from scratch.

By the time the two ladies sat at the table with their materials and their plates, their conversation had gone to another area, so they just enjoyed the delicious spaghetti, garlic bread, and fresh tossed salad with a glass of wine to wash it down. They decided they had plenty of time to handle the business of the worksheet after they had eaten and relaxed a bit after a full week of work. After all it was Friday, and they had no plans to go out on the town. A quiet night indoors was all they needed.

After an hour of shooting the breeze, Anastasia and Janice delved into the worksheet to see if they were on track with what they believed their calling to be. Below are the questions Dr. C. included on the worksheet and Anastasia's responses.

1. Listen to the desire in your heart. It is God who placed it in your heart for you to accomplish. What is your heart's desire? What motivates you more than anything?

This first question was easy for Anastasia to answer and had been since she was eight years old. Ever since Anastasia started school at four years of age, she was in love with the entire institution of education. By the time she had reached third grade, she was steadfastly determined to be an integral part of the educational system. Anytime she was approached as an adolescent with the age old question of "What do you want to be when you grow up?" she gave what had come to be her standard response: "I am going to be a teacher."

What motivated Anastasia to teach was being instrumental in the learning process. She loved watching the metaphorical light bulb go off. She had learned early on that listening was a large part of teaching. If she could listen and understand what a person did not comprehend when learning a set of specific information, she would be better able to fill in the missing pieces of information and get them on the right track.

In addition to being a teacher, Anastasia considers herself as a great motivator. She never sees life as a competition with others. She wants everyone she comes in contact with to be the best he/she can be by excelling in what he/she does.

2. In what way does your desire serve humanity or yourself?

The Bible say in Hosea 4:6a, *"My people are destroyed for lack of knowledge."* Anastasia presently teaches in two arenas: secular and spiritual. In the secular arena, she strives to equip people to become better communicators, so they can be better prepared for their professions and more efficient in their personal lives. In the spiritual arena, as a Bible instructor, Anastasia's attention is on the afterlife, attending to the eternity of souls. As a minister, she takes a personal responsibility to ensure people are *not* ignorant of Satan's devices (II Corinthians 2:11).

To do her part in evangelizing the world and preaching the gospel, Anastasia preaches the gospel as often as she can, teaches Bible classes (thematically and chapter by chapter, book by book), hosts an Internet-based Christian talk show, and writes Holy Spirit inspired faith-based books. She realizes she cannot be everywhere at all times, so her books and TV show are designed to gain a wider net than she can do in person.

When considering the latter part of the question- whether or not the desire served herself- she had to stop and ponder. In all honesty, Anastasia had to admit that there was a sense of accomplishment each time she witnessed the light bulb go off for a person she was teaching. But, she also had to admit that the person's enlightenment did not boost her ego. Rather, it gave her a sense of enjoyment because the person was closer to reaching his/her goal, and she was always truly humbled to have been a part of the journey.

3. Is accomplishing your desire beyond you and requires God's hand? If so, how so?

This question also came easy for Anastasia to answer. She believed wholeheartedly that each and every gift she possessed was given to her by the Lord for His use. To demonstrate this belief, she seeks God's guidance in using the gifts He placed in her to ensure she is in His will. The Bible says in Psalm 37:23, *"The steps of a good man are ordered by the Lord: and he delighteth in his way."* She desires to never make a misstep when it comes to using her gifts and talents. She never wants to be misconstrued as doing something for personal gain. Yes, she is aware she has to make a living, but she wants every decision and step to be ones of integrity.

4. Do you struggle to complete the task? Do you constantly need internal or external motivation?

After giving the question some thought, Anastasia was finally able to provide a sensible answer. First of all, from her own perspective, there is no sense of struggle when a task is presented to

Anastasia. Her first action is to always come up with a viable plan. After all, the Bible instructs us to write the vision and make it plain (Habakkuk 2:2). After constructing the plan, Anastasia solicits any assistance she may need. Afterward, she goes into the execution stage. While in this lengthy stage of the process, Anastasia keeps her eyes on the goal. Bringing the project to completion and checking it off her "to do" list is Anastasia's total and complete motivation.

5. Do you try to replicate someone's style or are you comfortable creating your own?

Psalm 139:14 says, *"I will praise thee; for I am fearfully and wonderfully made: marvellous are thy works; and that my soul knoweth right well."*

I Peter 2:9 says, *"But ye are a chosen generation, a royal priesthood, an holy nation, a peculiar people; that ye should shew forth the praises of him who hath called you out of darkness into his marvellous light. "*

Anastasia proclaims she is comfortable in her skin and expressing her own style. And she encourages others to do the same. Her belief is if someone attempts to emulate another person's style, that person is not confident with who he/she is. No one can effectively be another person. God designed each of us uniquely, and we should all strive to be the best person we can be. Moreover, if we stop competing with one another, we can help each other strengthen our weaknesses and hone our skills.

~~~~~~~~~~

After Anastasia and Janice completed their respective lists, they passed them to one another to peruse even though they had just discussed the answers aloud. A few minutes later, they both found themselves laughing. Before Anastasia could open her mouth, Janice said, "Girl, I can definitely say you are honest about who you say you are. I can attest to every word you said here," as she handed Anastasia her list back.

Anastasia laughed at Janice's assessment of her. "Well, you know one of my life's missions is to get everyone to do a self-examination. So, how would it seem if I failed to do my own?"

"Well, that makes perfect sense. No one can say you don't know your strengths and weaknesses. What did you think about my responses? Are they written clearly?"

Before answering, Anastasia tilted her head to the side and looked at her friend intently. "Yes, your responses are written clearly. I must say, you have a good handle on yourself as well, and I'm honored to know you."

Anastasia's response caught Janice off guard. "Why do you say that?" she asked surprised by her friend's compliment. No one had ever said those words to her before.

"Which part?"

"The part about being honored to know me."

"Not many people are as candid as you are and comfortable with themselves enough to state their shortcomings. And, on top of that," Anastasia continued, "you keep people at the forefront of your mission, by placing their needs above your own."

"Thank you for saying that," Janice said. "That means a lot to me. I try to live by Jesus' words 'Love thy neighbor.'"

"Girl, you're welcome. That is why I am proud to know you. Most people try to step on or over whomever they need to in order to get where they are trying to go."

"Yes, I know, but that is such a sad existence. People who live like that will surely reap what they sow."

"Yes, that is what the Word says."

The two women ended their evening with plans to meet soon, and Anastasia departed to make her way home. She had thoroughly enjoyed being in her friend's company. As far as she was concerned, they didn't do it often enough. However, she understood life is about balance: a healthy mixture of work and pleasure. Tonight, there was a good balance of each. With that thought, Anastasia smiled as she entered the freeway to make her way home.

~ ~ ~ ~ ~ ~ ~ ~ ~

That night, as Anastasia prepared for bed, she reflected on the first three steps of the process Dr. C. had illuminated in her workshop and accompanying materials. Anastasia could not say she had learned anything new about herself, but she was excited because she had remembered how God's hand was upon so much of what she had done- when she refrained from leaning to her own understanding, preventing her personal choices and desires to cloud her judgment and get in the way of God's plan.

Once Anastasia had arrived home, she prepared her clothing and briefcase for work the next day. Janice had sent a bowl of spaghetti and all the fixings home with her, so she did not need to worry about she would take for lunch. After a long, hot shower, she prepared for bed.

After falling asleep, not much later, the dreams started. That time, instead of her being inside a building, she was standing outside. The door to the building was actually a double door made of wood and appeared to very heavy from where she was standing, which was at the base of a short set of steps that led to the door.

When she awoke, she sat upright in bed pondering the dream, wondering if the building could be what she thought it was.

Chapter Five
Lord, Order My Steps

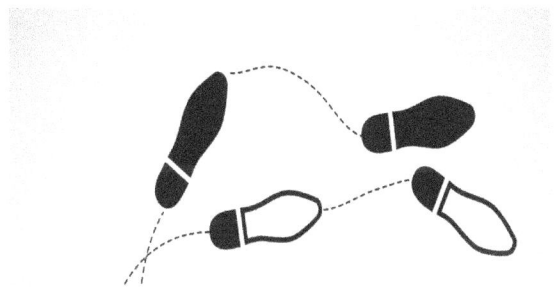

The next morning, as Anastasia thought back to Dr. C's seminar, she reflected on the second half of the day, when the participants returned after lunch. Dr. C. began to explain *Step Five: Receiving and Accepting God's Guidance.* She shared the following words of wisdom: After hearing God's voice giving you an assignment, the next action is to make sure you follow His direction every step of the way. Just because you have the assignment does not mean you know how to execute it. Therefore, if you can trust God to give you an assignment, you must trust Him to guide you from commencement to com-pletion. Psalm 37:23 says, *"The steps of a good man are ordered by the Lord: and he delighteth in his way."*

From the time God created man, He has been guiding them every step of the way. He does not give them an assignment and leave them alone to figure out what or how it must be done. Psalm 119:105 says, *"Thy word is a lamp unto my feet, and a light unto my path."* And, we are reminded in James 1:22, *"But be ye doers of the word, and not hearers only, deceiving your own selves."* Not only are we to heed the written Word of God, but the words He speaks to us: words of instruction. In doing so, we will have esteemed the words of His mouth more than our necessary food (Job 24:12). However, what constantly proves problematic is man's 'free-will agent' status. It has always been man's choice whether to receive and accept God's guidance. If we take to heart Isaiah 64:8, *"But now, O Lord, thou art our father; we are the clay, and thou our potter; and we all are the work of thy hand,"* we will understand that as His creation, He knows if we can handle the task and are capable of bringing it to completion. Therefore, we should trust in the Lord with all our heart and lean not to your own understanding (Proverbs 3:5-6).

After Dr. C's brief introduction of step five, she surprised the participants by asking them to form groups of ten to twelve persons and be ready for the instructions. Chairs were moved, and people positioned themselves around the tables instead of in the straight lines they had been in before. They were excited to see what the activity was and where it would lead.

Then, Dr. C. gave each group a person(s) in the Bible to discuss and outline. Specifically, Dr. C. wanted to know what instructions or assignment the person(s) was given, what guidance God provided, whether or not God's guidance was adhered to, and what the outcome was. The group Anastasia was assigned to was a lively bunch, and some of them proved to be very knowledgeable about the Bible.

The responses from each group are detailed below, to illustrate what they discovered about God's guidance and man's response. After reading these excerpts and seeing how God moves, you can then make a wise choice about how you will receive and respond to God's guidance.

Group One was given Adam and Eve. This is the response the team announcer gave to the listening audience (the other groups):

Chapter Two of the book of Genesis records the creation of humankind: man and woman. God fashioned the first man Adam from the dust of the ground and breathed life into him, and Adam became a living soul. Afterward, God placed Adam in the Garden of Eden. God instructed Adam that he was to till the ground and could eat freely of all the trees in the garden, except for the tree of the knowledge of good and evil. Later, God noticed Adam was not happy because each of the animals had both male and female, from which they could find a suitable mate, but Adam found no suitable mate for himself. There was no other creature like him.

Genesis 2:18 says, *"And the Lord God said, It is not good that the man should be alone; I will make him an help meet for him."* Subsequently, God caused Adam to fall into a deep sleep, meanwhile removing one of his ribs. Eve was then created from that rib to be Adam's companion. At that moment, they were innocent and unembarrassed about their nakedness. However, conditions would not remain calm in the garden. A serpent deceived Eve into eating fruit from the forbidden tree, and she gave some of the fruit to Adam.

Those acts gave them knowledge of good and evil, giving them the ability to conjure negative and destructive concepts, such as shame and evil. God later cursed the serpent for his actions and the ground. God had prophetically told the woman and the man what the consequences would be of their sin for disobeying God: they would surely die! Then, He banished them from the Garden of Eden. And, as God had promised- Adam and Eve died- spirituality- meaning from that point forward, they were disconnected from God due to their sin nature.

AND, the curse did not stop with them; it passed on to all of mankind, for the Bible says, "as by one man sin entered into the world..." (Romans 5:12).

Group Two was given Moses and focused on Numbers 20:1-12 to derive their response:

Then came the children of Israel, even the whole congregation, into the desert of Zin in the first month: and the people abode in Kadesh; and Miriam died there, and was buried there. And there was no water for the congregation: and they gathered themselves together against Moses and against Aaron. And the people chode with Moses, and spake, saying, Would God that we had died when our brethren died before the Lord! And why have ye brought up the congregation of the Lord into this wilderness, that we and our cattle should die there? And wherefore have ye made us to come up out of Egypt, to bring us in unto this evil place? it is no place of seed, or of figs, or of vines, or of pomegranates; neither is there any water to drink. And Moses and Aaron went from the presence of the assembly unto the door of the tabernacle of the congregation, and they fell upon their faces: and the glory of the Lord appeared unto them. And the Lord spake unto Moses, saying, Take the rod, and gather thou the assembly together, thou, and Aaron thy brother, and speak ye unto the rock before their eyes; and it shall give forth his water, and thou shalt bring forth to them water out of the rock: so thou shalt give the congregation and their beasts drink. And Moses took the rod from before the Lord, as he commanded him. And Moses and Aaron gathered the congregation together before the rock, and he said unto them, Hear now, ye rebels; must we fetch you water out of this rock? And Moses lifted up his hand, and with his rod he smote the rock twice: and the water came out abundantly, and the congregation drank, and their beasts also. And the Lord spake unto Moses and Aaron, Because ye believed me not, to sanctify me in the eyes of the children of Israel, therefore ye shall not bring this congregation into the land which I have given them.

God gave Moses a clear set of instructions that was designed to quell the murmuring and complaints of the Israelites who had been complaining about Moses' care for them from the time they had departed from Egypt. They believed they would have been better off if they had stayed put rather than leave the comfort of their domicile, even though they had been enslaved by the Egyptians. God specifically told Moses to speak to the rock, so God's power could be demonstrated through Moses. God wanted to show the Israelites He had not forgotten about them and He would take care of them as they traversed from Egypt to the land God had promised to their forefathers.

Regardless of God's specificity, Moses took matters into his own hands and struck the rock rather than speak to it. Yes, water did flow from it, but instead of God receiving the praise and adoration, it was diverted to Moses. God was displeased with Moses' action of disobedience. The resulting consequence was Moses was then prohibited from entered the Promised Land. God allowed him to see it, but he was not permitted to set his feet there.

When God gives specific orders, He does so for a reason. We may not understand His reasoning, but faith is not predicated upon our understanding. Rather, *"faith is the substance of things hoped for, the evidence of things not seen,"* Hebrews 11:1.

Group Three was given Joseph, Jacob's eleventh son. Joseph's story, recorded in Genesis 37–50, demonstrates what God can do for those who remain upright and faithful, despite their unfair treatment by others. Genesis 37:4 tells us, *"When his brothers saw that their father loved [Joseph] more than any of them, they hated him and could not speak a kind word to him."* Joseph was one of Jacob's twelve sons, and during his teenage years, Joseph's older brothers became jealous of him because their father loved him more. One day when Joseph went to check on their wellbeing, at their father's request, as they tended the flocks, his brothers assaulted him, stripped him of his coat of many colors, and sold him as a slave to a passing merchant.

Joseph was taken against his will to Egypt where he was purchased by one of Pharaoh's officials to become a house slave. Despite the radical change in his station and the betrayal by his brothers, Joseph did not turn away from God. In fact, he did the opposite: Joseph drew closer. He remained a righteous man throughout his ordeal, undeterred and godly. God honored Joseph's faithfulness by blessing his work in his Egyptian master's house.

Genesis 39:2–3 reads, *"The Lord was with Joseph and he prospered, and he lived in the house of his Egyptian master...the Lord gave him success in everything he did."* But Joseph's trials were not over. Later, and after he refused her sexual advances, the Egyptian master's wife made a false charge against Joseph. As a result, he was arrested and sent to Pharaoh's prison.

While Joseph was in prison, God intervened again. Genesis 39:20–21 declares, *"But while Joseph was there in the prison, the Lord was with him; he showed him kindness and granted him favor in the eyes of the prison warden."* The Lord was with Joseph in his Egyptian master's house (Gen. 39:2), and the Lord was with him in Pharaoh's prison (Genesis 39:20). After a series of God-directed events (Gen. 40–41), Pharaoh released Joseph from prison and appointed him as his second in command over all of Egypt.

Joseph went from betrayed brother to slave to national ruler, and all by the providence of God. God's plan from the beginning was to place Joseph in a position of authority in Egypt, and that is exactly what happened. With God's help, Joseph overcame all of the man-made obstacles in his path. Joseph consistently aligned with God, and God prevailed as He always does. God blessed Joseph by intervening in his life, and Joseph responded with respect, loyalty, and obedience. In the end and through his position as the ruler of all of Egypt, Joseph helped his brothers who had previously betrayed him. Joseph was a righteous man of God through and through from start to finish.

Group Four was given Abraham to assess. They elected to use the following verse as a foundation for their assessment coupled with Genesis 12:1-3, which provides all the details. Hebrews 11:8 declares, *By faith Abraham, when he was called to go out into a place which he should after receive for an inheritance, obeyed; and he went out, not knowing whither he went.*

Genesis 12:1-3 says, *Now the Lord had said unto Abram, Get thee out of thy country, and from thy kindred, and from thy father's house, unto a land that I will shew thee: And I will make of thee a great nation, and I will bless thee, and make thy name great; and thou shalt be a blessing: And I will bless them that bless thee, and curse him that curseth thee: and in thee shall all families of the earth be blessed. So Abram departed, as the Lord had spoken unto him; and Lot went with him: and Abram was seventy and five years old when he departed out of Haran.*

God called Abraham out from his home in Haran and told him to go to a land that He would show to him. God also made three promises to Abraham: 1) the promise of a land of his own; 2) the promise to be made into a great nation; and 3) the promise of blessing. Those promises form the basis for what would later be called the Abrahamic Covenant (established in Genesis 15 and ratified in Genesis 17). What really made Abraham special was that he obeyed God. Genesis 12:4 records that, after God called Abraham, he went "as the LORD had told him." That act of faith was so impressive that the author of Hebrews "enshrines" Abraham in the Faith Hall of Fame.

Another example of Abraham's life of faith is seen in the birth of his son, Isaac. Abraham and Sarah were childless, yet God promised Abraham would have a son (Genesis 15:4). The son would be not only the heir of Abraham's vast fortune with which God blessed him but, more importantly, the heir of promise and the continuation of the godly line of Seth. Abraham believed the promise of God, and it was credited to him as righteousness (Genesis 15:6).

God reiterated His promise to Abraham in Genesis 17, and his faith was rewarded, as recorded in Genesis 21, with the birth of Isaac. Again, the author of Hebrews highlights this when he writes, "*By faith Abraham, even though he was past age—and Sarah herself was barren—was enabled to become a father because he considered him faithful who had made the promise. And so from this one man, and he as good as dead, came descendants as numerous as the stars in the sky and as countless as the sand on the seashore"* (Hebrews 11:11-12).

Abraham's faith was sorely tested regarding his son, Isaac. In Genesis 22, God commanded Abraham to sacrifice Isaac on the top of Mount Moriah. We don't know how Abraham reacted internally to the command. What we do know is this- As with the earlier command to leave his home and family, Abraham obeyed (Genesis 22:3). And, we know the story ends with God holding back Abraham from sacrificing Isaac. Imagine how Abraham must have felt. He had been waiting decades for a son of his own, and the God who promised the child to him was about to take him away.

The point is that Abraham's faith in God was greater than his love for his son, and he trusted that even if he sacrificed Isaac, God was able to bring him back from the dead (Hebrews 11:17-19).

Group Five was given Joseph, the husband of Mary, Jesus' mother.

Matthew 1:18-25 gives the following account of Joseph's actions: *Now the birth of Jesus Christ was on this wise: When as his mother Mary was espoused to Joseph, before they came together, she was found with child of the Holy Ghost. Then Joseph her husband, being a just man, and not willing to make her a public example, was minded to put her away privily. But while he thought on these things, behold, the angel of the Lord appeared unto him in a dream, saying, Joseph, thou son of David, fear not to take unto thee Mary thy wife: for that which is conceived in her is of the Holy Ghost. And she shall bring forth a son, and thou shalt call his name Jesus: for he shall save his people from their sins. Now all this was done, that it might be fulfilled which was spoken of the Lord by the prophet, saying, Behold, a virgin shall be with child, and shall bring forth a son, and they shall call his name Emmanuel, which being interpreted is, God with us. Then Joseph being raised from sleep did as the angel of the Lord had bidden him, and took unto him his wife: And knew her not till she had brought forth her firstborn son: and he called his name Jesus.*

During that crucial time in Mary's life and consequently Joseph's life, Joseph had a decision to make. He could go with his first mind and separate himself from Mary, preventing his involvement in any scandal that could ensue. Or, he could do as directed by the angel of the Lord. Being the man of God that he was, Joseph did as the angel directed him. We are not told what happened as a direct result, as far as rumors or his reputation are concerned, but there is one thing we know for sure: what God had set in motion was going to come to pass. God had chosen Mary to be Jesus' mother and Joseph to be His earthly father. If Joseph had "put her away privily," he would not have stood in the position of "father." Joseph obeyed the voice of the Lord and put his trust in Him, knowing He knows what is best.

Group Six discussed the pillars of cloud and fire that guided the Israelites. Exodus 13:21-22 says, *"And the Lord went before them by day in a pillar of a cloud, to lead them the way; and by night in a pillar of fire, to give them light; to go by day and night: He took not away the pillar of the cloud by day, nor the pillar of fire by night, from before the people."*

The pillar of cloud by day and the pillar of fire by night guided the Israelites during their exodus from Egyptian bondage. This allowed them to travel by day and by night. Exodus 13:21-22 explains that God gave them the pillar of cloud by day to lead them in the way He wanted them to go and the pillar of fire by night to give light. The pillar was not just symbolism but a real phenomenon. We have no way of knowing how God made the pillar, but it was obviously a miraculous event that God used to lead them for their forty years in the wilderness. During the day, the pillar guided their journey. During the night, it gave light and, no doubt, comfort.

From the six group explanations provided above, we can discern that God leads us by a variety of methods. The method God chooses to lead us is not as important or critical as our response. As stated at the beginning of the chapter, if we can trust God's voice to give us an assignment, we should have a same level of trust to receive His guidance to see the assignment to completion. Jeremiah 29:11 says, *"For I know the thoughts that I think toward you, saith the Lord, thoughts of peace, and not of evil, to give you an expected end."*

Chapter Six
Bringing the Assignment to a Close

In the last couple of hours of Dr. C's seminar, Anastasia's excitement continued to grow from everything she had heard thus far. She felt a spiritual awakening with all the information she had been given and the activities she had engaged in that day. But, when Dr. C. discussed the fifth component of her "Time is Running Out" workshop: *Completing the Task at Hand*, Anastasia felt a wave of emotions, including both sadness and excitement. Most importantly though, she found a deeper sense of understanding the importance of completing one's God-given assignments.

To drive the point home for the attendees, Dr. C. used our savior, the Lord Jesus Christ, as the supreme example. Listening to our Savior's plight and how he was mistreated is what caused Anastasia sadness. But His victory in defeating the enemy, His sin sacrifice, and the illustration that His life serves for all believers is what brought her joy, hope, and excitement.

Dr. C's illustration went as such:

There is no one who enters into the earth realm that is void of purpose. Each person who is born is given a destiny, which he/she is to fulfill. Jesus, our Lord and Savior, is a perfect example. Due to the fallen nature of man and his separation from God, sacrifices had been made in an attempt to blot out sin, thereby redeeming humanity. However, the blood of animals was insufficient in permanently blotting out man's sin or redeeming mankind back to the Creator. Only another human, one who was blameless, unspotted, and pure, could stand as a human sacrifice for all humanity.

Hebrews 10:5-7 declares with power, *"Wherefore when he cometh into the world, he saith, Sacrifice and offering thou wouldest not, but a body hast thou prepared me: In burnt offerings and sacrifices for sin thou hast had no pleasure. Then said I, Lo, I come (in the volume of the book it is written of me,) to do thy will, O God."*

Jesus was explaining that God the Father was not pleased with animal sacrifices as an attempt to blot out sin, so He prepared a body for Jesus, to leave His heavenly home and enter into the earth realm, to fulfill the requirement no other human could fulfill. And, Jesus willingly accepted the task. He left His home of glory, stepping out of eternity and into time.

And He said He comes in the *volume* of the book, meaning he comes in the entirety of the Holy Script, the book that speaks of Him, the book that prophesied His coming through a virgin birth and His subsequent death by crucifixion.

This is Jesus's story: Mary, a teenage virgin, experienced the presence of an angel, who told her that the Holy Spirit would come upon her, and as a result, she would be impregnated with the Savior of the world. Nine months later, she gave birth to a son, and His earthly father Joseph named him Jesus, also known as Emmanuel, God with us. Jesus lived a sheltered and protected life, but at the age of 30, He began his public ministry, by going to the Jordan River and being baptized by his forerunner John the Baptist. Prior to that time, His brothers would taunt Him by telling Him to let people know who He was, but He would tell them that His time had not yet come. He was sensitive to the voice of God, and He was determined not to move until God said so.

Like Jesus, we need to be aware of the right moment to move in our assignment. We must be careful not to go before God says the timing is right, nor must we belabor the point. Jesus was already aware of His assignment, but He waited until God the father gave Him the go ahead to commence His earthly assignment. Although this time had been prophesied, the way had to be made straight. God had placed a forerunner in position to prepare Jesus' way. God does the same for us; He places events and/or people before us who will either lay a foundation or clear debris from our path before we are even placed on it.

After Jesus was baptized, He had to further consecrate Himself for ministry. Matthew 4:1-11 shares the account:

"Then was Jesus led up of the Spirit into the wilderness to be tempted of the devil. And when he had fasted forty days and forty nights, he was afterward an hungred. And when the tempter came to him, he said, If thou be the Son of God, command that these stones be made bread. But he answered and said, It is written, Man shall not live by bread alone, but by every word that proceedeth out of the mouth of God. Then the devil taketh him up into the holy city, and setteth him on a pinnacle of the temple, And saith unto him, If thou be the Son of God, cast thyself down: for it is written, He shall give his angels charge concerning thee: and in their hands they shall bear thee up, lest at any time thou dash thy foot against a stone. Jesus said unto him, It is written again, Thou shalt not tempt the Lord thy God. Again, the devil taketh him up into an exceeding high mountain, and sheweth him all the kingdoms of the world, and the glory of them; And saith unto him, All these things will I give thee, if thou wilt fall down and worship me. Then saith Jesus unto him, Get thee hence, Satan: for it is written, Thou shalt worship the Lord thy God, and him only shalt thou serve. Then the devil leaveth him, and, behold, angels came and ministered unto him."

Satan will come to tempt us at various stages throughout our journey, while we are on assignment, but we must stay focused on the goal. He will usually come when we are at our weakest moments, trying to distract us from the task at hand. Satan approached Jesus when Jesus was physically weak from not having eaten natural food for forty days. Nevertheless, Jesus found the strength to ward off Satan's advances. We too must be strong.

James 4:7 instructs us to *"Submit yourselves therefore to God. Resist the devil, and he will flee from you."*

Jesus resisted Satan, and eventually Satan went away. Afterward, Jesus went about doing good in the land and ministering to all He came in contact with. Because He was doing good, Satan set various snares to throw Jesus off course. Jesus stayed steadfast and unmovable, abounding in the work of His father. We must exert the same focus and tenacity about the assignment God places in our hands.

Finally, after three and a half years of ministry, the time came where Jesus found Himself at the end of the journey, and it was time for the task to be completed. After He had dinner with His disciples in the upper room (the Last Supper), He made His way to the garden of Gethsemane to pray.

> Matthew 26:36 tells us what occurs next in Jesus' story,
> *"Then cometh Jesus with them unto a place called Gethsemane, and saith unto the disciples, Sit ye here, while I go and pray yonder. And he took with him Peter and the two sons of Zebedee, and began to be sorrowful and very heavy. Then saith he unto them, My soul is exceeding sorrowful, even unto death: tarry ye here, and watch with me. And he went a little further, and fell on his face, and prayed, saying, O my Father, if it be possible, let this cup pass from me: nevertheless not as I will, but as thou wilt. And he cometh unto the disciples, and findeth them asleep, and saith unto Peter, What, could ye not watch with me one hour? Watch and pray, that ye enter not into temptation: the spirit indeed is willing, but the flesh is weak. He went away again the second time, and prayed, saying, O my Father, if this cup may not pass away from me, except I drink it, thy will be done. And he came and found them asleep again: for their eyes were heavy. And he left them, and went away again, and prayed the third time, saying the same words. Then cometh he to his disciples, and saith unto them, Sleep on now, and take your rest: behold, the hour is at hand, and the Son of man is betrayed into the hands of sinners. Rise, let us be going: behold, he is at hand that doth betray me.*
> *And while he yet spake, lo, Judas, one of the twelve, came, and with him a great multitude with swords and staves, from the chief priests and elders of the people. Now he that betrayed him gave them a sign, saying, Whomsoever I shall kiss, that same is he: hold him fast. And forthwith he came to Jesus, and said, Hail, master; and kissed him. And Jesus said unto him, Friend, wherefore art thou come? Then came they, and laid hands on*

Jesus, and took him. And, behold, one of them which were with Jesus stretched out his hand, and drew his sword, and struck a servant of the high priest's, and smote off his ear. Then said Jesus unto him, Put up again thy sword into his place: for all they that take the sword shall perish with the sword. Thinkest thou that I cannot now pray to my Father, and he shall presently give me more than twelve legions of angels? But how then shall the scriptures be fulfilled, that thus it must be? In that same hour said Jesus to the multitudes, Are ye come out as against a thief with swords and staves for to take me? I sat daily with you teaching in the temple, and ye laid no hold on me. But all this was done, that the scriptures of the prophets might be fulfilled. Then all the disciples forsook him, and fled."

When the time came for Jesus to move into the final stage of God's plan, He was left on His own without His loyal followers. There will be people in your life who are only going to walk so far with you on your journey, and in the moment you find crucial, they will leave you to face the battle on your own. Do not become dismayed because God did not call them for the task. He called you! Therefore, you are the only one who is required to stand in the midst of that circumstance.

Jesus was arrested and eventually stood trial, at which He was *not* found guilty of any crimes. But after a decision of whether to release Jesus of Nazareth or Barabbas, the crowd chose Barabbas, a known murderer to be released instead of an innocent man. But remember, God was at work.

Eventually, Jesus was stripped of His clothing and a crown of thorns was pressed into His temple. He was scourged (beaten with a whip, often referred to as a cat-of-nine-tales). Then, after being thoroughly ridiculed and seemingly humiliated, He was made to carry His cross up Golgotha Hill, the hill of skulls. Eventually, due to His physical weakness, as He was in the body of a mere mortal, He had to have assistance in carrying the weighty cross.

Having reached His destination, He was subsequently hung upon His cross, between two malefactors, with nails driven through the palms of His hands and through His ankles, but none of His bones were broken. While on the cross, Jesus spoke seven sayings; one of which *was "Eli, Eli, lama sabachthani? that is to say, My God, my God, why hast thou forsaken me?"* (Matthew 27:45). *"After this, Jesus knowing that all things were now accomplished, that the scripture might be fulfilled, saith, I thirst. Now there was set a vessel full of vinegar: and they filled a spunge with vinegar, and put it upon hyssop, and put it to his mouth. When Jesus therefore had received the vinegar, he said, It is finished: and he bowed his head, and gave up the ghost"* (John 19:28-30).

Jesus, as the unspotted lamb, took the punishment that rightfully belonged to a sinful generation, in order to redeem this same generation back to God. The task wasn't easy because of all the obstacles and physical suffering Jesus had to encounter, but He did it willingly. Once He set His feet onto the path, there was no retreating. There was no back peddling. There was no giving up. We must be that dedicated to our assignment.

When Dr. C. asked the attendees how many of them could say they were truly dedicated to their assignment, hands went up all over the room, as tears streamed down many of their faces. Some of them even went to the front of the room to be prayed for, essentially rededicating themselves to God for His use, rendering themselves as willing vessels.

~~~~~~~~~

That night, Anastasia found it difficult to fall asleep once again. It wasn't that she was nervous or upset about anything. It was quite the contrary. She was excited about the changes God was making in her life. He was unfolding her dreams right before her eyes. She could literally feel the shift taking place. She desperately wanted to know all God had in store for her, but she knew she needed to exercise patience. She was truly overjoyed that God would allow her dreams to come true. She understood He was strategically putting all the pieces in place. She was in awe of God's majesty!

When Anastasia finally drifted off to sleep, after turning on one of her favorite television shows that she used the voices of the actors to distract her thoughts until she fell asleep, she eventually ventured into the dream state.

Anastasia woke up early the next morning at 5 AM, with a smile on her face and tears wetting her pillow. Once again, she had the dream regarding the building. That time, she found herself standing outside on the steps once again, facing the front of the building. She noticed something quite interesting and was not sure if it had been there before in the last dream. To her surprise, there was a name across the top of the building, above the doors. Then, on the right side of the door, positioned slightly below the name was another name, with the word *Founder* printed underneath.

The first name was the name she had given to the school she desires to build. The second name on the right side of the door above founder was her name.

As Anastasia replayed the dream over and over in her mind, the tears continued to flow. She knelt down on her knees and gave God praise.

Chapter Seven
A New Assignment

We are constantly growing and changing in our spiritual life, if and only if we continue to develop our relationship with Christ, our Savior. We should be maturing and becoming more like Christ. To do this, we must study His Word, to know His likes and dislikes and ultimately, His expectations.

As we mature, we will be given new spiritual assignments that we can handle that we could not handle before due to spiritual immaturity in that area. These assignments are given because God is preparing you for even greater things.

As Anastasia had listened on Dr. C.'s words, she automatically reflected on her own life and the assignments God had given her over the years. When she first became serious about ministry, God allowed her to participate in church events by sharing the announcements. Then, God moved her to reading scripture. Next, she began to give exhortations and pray. Then, she moved to teaching Bible study and other classes. Now, she ministers the Word of God twice a month. A person could view the development of advancement this way: positions and duties change when vacancies occur. Or, it can be viewed this way: God knew the vacancies would occur, creating a need, so He prepared someone to fill the void.

Daniel gives us a glimpse into the character and nature of God. He shows how God changes our assignments. Daniel 2:21 says, *"He controls the course of world events; he removes kings and sets up other kings. He gives wisdom to the wise and knowledge to the scholars."* Here, we see God not only controls the course of events in our life but is willing to give wisdom and knowledge to us. Because God does give us wisdom and knowledge about the changes in our lives, you can be sure that you have everything you need to move to your next level. You have enough to make the shift.

Dr. C. shared the following ten principles to assist you in moving into your next God-given assignment. She credits Pastor Duke Taber, the senior pastor at The Vineyard Church in San Carlos, CA, for the steps although she adapted them. He shared them online for those whom God calls.

1. *Be Convinced God is Calling You*

When God begins to move and take you through a transition, it is important that you are thoroughly convinced He is calling you to your next endeavor. You need to be secure in His plans and purposes for your life as best as you understand them. When you know deep down inside your heart that God has called you to the next adventure in Him, then nothing can convince you otherwise. You know that it is God's destiny for you and that you would be walking outside of the will of God if you did not follow it.

The reason that this is important is because there will be times that this belief will be tested. If you are not convinced, then every time you hit a snag, encounter a trial, run into a roadblock, you will focus on the problem and will give up on the assignment, believing maybe God did not call you after all. That my friend is a trick of the enemy. He does not want you or God to succeed in any plan you may have.

You will not overcome your challenges and pursue your destiny because your lack of conviction will lead you to abandon the mission to which God has called you. There are many times when only your conviction of your call will be what you can draw on when facing hardships.

If you are going to deal with change effectively and persevere through those hardships, you have to be convinced that you are walking according to the call that you have received. You have to be so convinced that no matter what happens, you will not quit. The conviction in your heart that God has called you to this transition and change will birth in you the determination to succeed regardless of personal cost.

2. *Don't Rely on Prophetic Words Alone*

Prophetic words alone are not meant to give you direction but instead work in conjunction with what the Holy Spirit is already doing in your life. In other words, the prophetic word comes to confirm what God has already spoken to you in another form. Do not pack your bags just because you received a prophetic word out of the blue. In the book of Acts we have an account of the Apostle Paul receiving a prophetic word. Acts 21:10-12: *"Several days later a man named Agabus, who also had the gift of prophecy, arrived from Judea. He came over, took Paul's belt, and bound his own feet and hands with it. Then he said, 'The Holy Spirit declares, "So shall the owner of this belt be bound by the Jewish leaders in Jerusalem and turned over to the Gentiles."' When we heard this, we and the local believers all begged Paul not to go on to Jerusalem."*

Here, we see that Paul was given a prophetic word from a man named Agabus. Those that heard this word assumed it was a word to warn Paul not to go. However, Paul knew what it meant because the Holy Spirit had already been dealing with him previously. Acts 22:22-24: *"And now I am bound by the Spirit to go to Jerusalem. I don't know what awaits me, except that the Holy Spirit tells me in city after city that jail and suffering lie ahead. But my life is worth nothing to me unless I use it for finishing the work assigned me by the Lord Jesus - the work of telling others the Good News about the wonderful grace of God."* For Paul, the word of prophecy that was given to him by Agabus was not a word of warning but a word of confirmation about what he was sensing would lie ahead. It was actually a word of encouragement to Him that God knew the trials that were ahead and that God was preparing his heart to face them.

3. *Understand the Path You Have Traveled to See the Path You Are to Follow*

When you are moving into your next spiritual assignment, God builds upon what He has done with you in the past. He builds His temple in you line upon line and precept upon precept (Isaiah 28:10). As you go down your journey in life, you can look back and see patterns of what God has done to get an idea of what He is doing.

Take a moment to look back upon your life. See your past involvement and experiences—whether in ministry, in education, in social settings, or in a professional capacity—as training grounds. View those experiences as places where God has prepared you. He has been equipping you for the next level. God will expand you in those specific areas or build upon the foundation that is already in you. Anastasia found that statement to be true. Professionally, she has served in the capacity as educator for 24 years plus another 16 years before that (her pre-service years that started from age eight).

Then, the discussion truly turned interesting when Dr. C. stated, "Don't forget to look at your past failures and pain. God even uses those experiences to prepare you for your future." Although it sounded a little absurd, Anastasia knew the words to be true, for God turns messes into messages and trials into testimonies.

4. *Evaluate the Changes You Must Make*

Many times we think we just need to pray more, read our Bible more, or worship more to be prepared for the next assignment God will give us. All of these things are good and part of the process, but they are not the *only* part of the process. There are non-spiritual things that we need to do as well. There are certain specifics that God will begin to prepare you in for your next assignment that are not tied to His preparation in the past or how spiritually prepared you are.

As you sense Him leading you to the next level and begin to discern specifics about the new assignment, you will enter into a different kind of preparation. It involves the practical changes you need to make in your life in order to actually fulfill the new assignment or embrace the new season God has for you. These things might include eliminating any financial debt you might have, so you can live on a salary that is less than you had before. It might be tying up loose ends where you are now, so you are free to go to where He is leading you. It may mean allowing Him to break emotional attachments you currently have in order for you to establish new attachments in your new assignment. Evaluate what has to be changed in the natural world and allow God to start changing those things in your life.

This step really spoke volumes to Anastasia as the building she continuously dreamed about flashed in her mind. The revelation hit her like a ton of bricks. She had a longing desire to own and operate a school. In the last few months, God had been really moving in her life to make her dream become a reality, and she felt His presence as He guided her step by step. Hearing the details of this step was definitely confirmation for Anastasia that she was on her way to another God-given assignment.

5. Be Prepared to Overcome Opposition

Just because God has called you to do something does not mean it will be easy. No great man or woman of God was exempt from opposition. Even Jesus was opposed by the devil, religious leaders, and at times even His friends and family. You need to commit to overcoming opposition. Know that the changes will have their challenges, and make a proactive decision to emerge victoriously, by God's grace, in every way.

One of the greatest barriers to moving forward to the next level is being too comfortable functioning where you are. You may want something different, but when you move into it, you realize the new assignment has no respect whatsoever for your comfort zone. It will stretch you, challenge you, and be full of experiences that are unfamiliar to you.

Some people encounter physical opposition, are thrown in jail, and are persecuted for their faith. However, most of the opposition we will encounter is less dramatic. Most of it will come in subtle ways that attempt to sidetrack us with the cares of this world. It is this opposition you must first overcome before you will ever be faced with overcoming the more dramatic kind.

As Anastasia listened to the details of this step, she thought about how many times she warned herself to not be sidetracked by negativity because it is a tool Satan uses to distract those God is calling. She wants to keep her mind, heart, and ears clear from debris.

6. *Find a Mentor to Help You Move to Your Next Spiritual Level*

The kingdom of God is not built by lone rangers, and great men and women of God are not born that way. They become that way through the influence of other great believers in their lives. Barnabas mentored Paul, and Paul mentored Timothy, Titus, and Epaphroditus. The wisdom and knowledge that a mentor can give to you is invaluable. Having a mentor to walk with you and help you mature in your ministry will allow you to fail without doubting God's call. It will also help you learn from your mistakes as you walk with someone who has the experience, wisdom, and ability to help you grow and develop. Proper alignment with a mentor is not only a great source of guidance and support, it can also be crucial to the fulfillment of your destiny and vital to your getting to the next level.

Anastasia quickly thought back over her life to see if she had any mentors in the educational arena. She had plenty spiritual mentors. Of course, she could never forget her third grade teacher, Mrs. Joan Coleman. She had inspired Anastasia greatly, but that was in the classroom, not as a business owner, a CEO of a school. Then, she thought of Mrs. Barbara Carroll, who was once the principal of a private Christian school that was owned by a church. Later, Mrs. Carroll opened her own school. Anastasia had always thought of her over the years and had even tried looking for her phone number on line or going by her school. She was unsuccessful in her attempts, but she was not opposed to trying again. She believes Mrs. Carroll will be a great mentor.

7. *Understand That Spiritual Attacks Will Come*

The more you walk into the plans and purposes God has for you, the more you will come under enemy fire. You become a threat to the kingdom of darkness, and because of that, you become a target. Understand that this is normal and not somehow a sign that you are missing the mark. Many people think that when spiritual attacks come, it signifies they are doing something wrong. On the contrary, the exact opposite is true. You are doing something right!

Even though we know the enemy of our souls is defeated, there is still a battle raging, and we must expect to be attacked when we are making advances into areas he is controlling. The attacks of our opposition seem to intensify when we move from one level to the next. Whenever we embrace a new season or take on a new assignment, warfare follows because the enemy wants to stop us from doing what we are called to do to advance God's kingdom.

You are probably accustomed to the level of warfare you have experienced in your current circumstances, but you need to know that when you step up, the battles will heat up. Even though the battle may heat up and become fiercer as you advance into the next season in your life, remember our basic weaponry remains the same. In Christ, you have spiritual armor to protect against the attacks of the enemy (Eph. 6:13-18).

You also have the weapon of His Word, the power of His Spirit, and the reinforcement of other believers. Use everything available to you as a Christian, and though attacks will come, you will overcome with God's help.

8. *God Chose to Call You to This Spiritual Assignment- Accept It!*

Many times as we enter into our new assignment from the Lord, we are tempted to feel overwhelmed. It seems so much bigger than what we are capable of or deserve even. Remember, it was not your choice that put you there; it was His choice. God enables those He calls. Learn to accept the decision was ultimately God's and not yours. With that choice and call comes an anointing and an authority that you haven't experienced before. It comes to you because of His grace, not your merit. At the same time, don't walk in false humility. God did call you. Accept that decision.

As you are settling in to your new place, you must resist the temptation to be shy, sheepish, or apologetic about what God has done in you. Be gracious, of course, but do not let false humility creep into your thoughts or conversation. A genuinely humble person accepts and acknowledges what God has done in his/her life. If you want to live in true humility, do not try to explain away God's work in your life. Instead, be honest about what He is doing, admit your need for His grace, and give Him glory without being pious.

God calls all types of people to different tasks and different roles. One is not greater than the other. Everyone is given the grace and ability to perform those tasks and walk in those roles. As you simply trust His wisdom and follow His lead, your confidence and anointing will continue to increase.

Do not become proud, but neither should you deny who God has designed you to be.

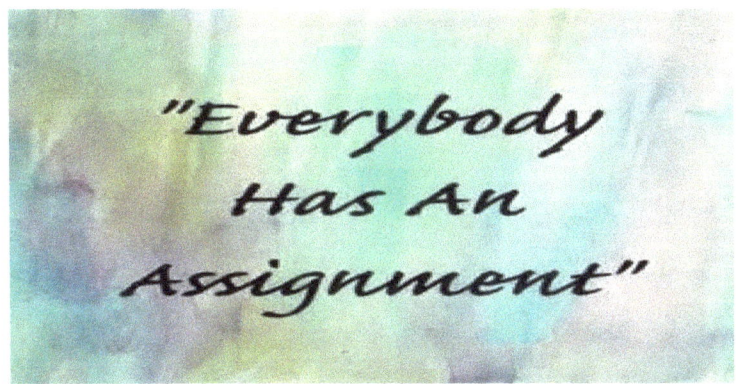

9. *Change is a Process not an Event*

Haste makes waste and wounds souls. Be patient in your transition to your next level. God is not in a hurry. He wants to allow people time to process the changes He is making. He cares about their souls and wants them to come along in the journey. I want to encourage you now to determine to be patient as you move into your new season. Do not try to change things for yourself too quickly or rush ahead of God's timing. God has designed change to be a process, not an event.

He is certainly interested in the result of the changes He orchestrates in our lives, but the process of growth and maturity that accompanies change is also very important to Him. For this reason, He typically works diligently, deliberately, and more slowly than you might want!

However, you need to remember that His timing is perfect; it is part of a grand plan for your life. In addition, it will bring you great joy and fulfillment as you patiently cooperate with it. The Christian life is a journey. Part of that experience is what you learn as you walk along the path. Too many times in our society we expect instant results to go along with our instant potatoes. God just does not work that way. He is building our lives piece by piece. If you rush the process, then there will be weaknesses that you will have to deal with later because you did not allow God to place into your life all the pieces you need. You will be like a house without half of the 2x4's in the walls holding the walls in place.

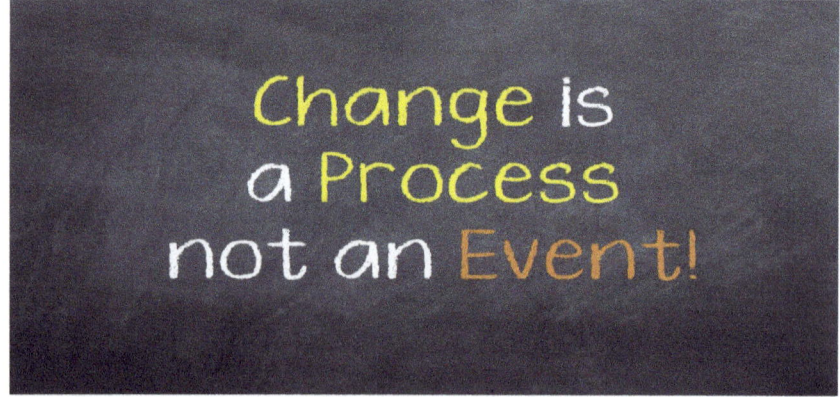

10. *Be Bold, Be Strong, for the Lord Your God is With You*

Any time you are going to move forward with God, there comes a time when you finally have to go for it. You have to take that step of faith. This is the step beyond commitment, the step beyond decision making; it is the step of no return. It is when you finally put action to your calling. The Apostle James put it this way: *"For as the body without the spirit is dead, so faith without works is dead also"* (James 2:26).

Step out boldly into your new calling. You can study, commit, decide, until the cows come home, but if you do not step out in faith, it is all for nothing. Jesus is saying to you: *"Come on! Take that step of bold faith. I am ready and waiting to walk with you."*

Always remember, God is faithful. He who began a good work in you will be faithful to complete it (Phil. 1:6). Move on, and move up.

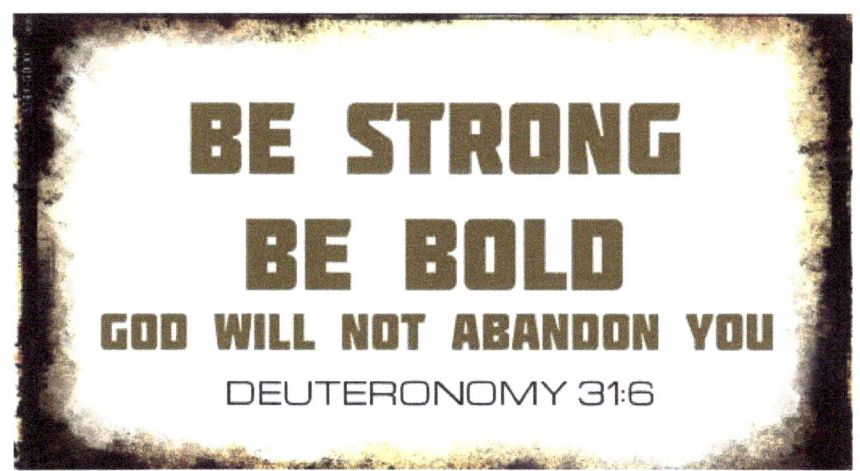

As you complete one assignment, you must spiritually prepare for the next. The Lord will order your steps and equip you for the journey ahead. Trust the Lord in what He has entrusted to you, for He knows the abilities you possess. After all, He equipped you with them.

Some assignments may be more exhilarating than others, while others may be more arduous or time consuming than the one before. Regardless of the type of assignment, complete it with joy.

Remember, the Lord loves a cheerful giver, so give with your whole heart and remember to smile!

Chapter Eight
Final Thoughts

God has called every believer to work for Him. He has prepared us to take on a specific assignment. Furthermore, He has given us the tools we need to complete it. Now, He is waiting for us to take up the reigns and step up to the task. Sure, we may have moments when we feel inadequate, and perhaps, we even wonder if we actually heard His voice. Satan, the deceiver, wants us to doubt who we are in Christ. He wants us to be unsettled and ambivalent about our decisions. If the enemy can throw us off course, God's plan will remain uncompleted.

Don't be a pawn in the enemy's scheme. Take a step of faith and trust the voice you heard or the feeling you have deep in your soul. Be confident about who God has created you to be.

To get to that point, it may take you reading your Word more and spending more time with the Lord, to ensure you know His voice and His plan for your life. It may even take reading this book over and over again, until you know without a shadow of doubt who you are in Christ.

If as a child you heard negativity about the life you would lead as an adult, that stigma may still be attached to you. Do not allow the voices of naysayers to dictate your life. God is the one who created you, and He knows the plans He has for you. *"For I know the thoughts that I think toward you, saith the Lord, thoughts of peace, and not of evil, to give you an expected end"* (Jeremiah 29:11).

To rid yourself of those negative thoughts and words that constantly ring in your ears, you must cancel Satan's assignment over your life. God said He would rebuke the devourer. *"And I will rebuke the devourer for your sakes, and he shall not destroy the fruits of your ground; neither shall your vine cast her fruit before the time in the field, saith the Lord of hosts"* (Malachi 3:11). To walk in God's promises, each stipulation must be filled. So, read Malachi 3:8-10, to understand the conditions that have been set forth to ensure you qualify.

The Lord loves you and wants the best for you. Do not allow the enemy to trick you to live your life in vain, by not fulfilling your greatest potential and using your God-given talents. If you are unsure of what to do and how to do it, do not fret. For, the Lord will be your guide. He will be with you every step of the way!

Gift of Salvation for Non-Believers

"For all have sinned, and come short of the glory of God."
*(*Romans 3:23)

This section was written especially for non-believers, those who have not accepted the gift of salvation. The gift of salvation saves souls from eternal damnation and is a free gift offered by God himself.

John 3:16-18 says, *"For God so loved the world, that he gave his only begotten Son, that whosoever believeth in him should not perish, but have everlasting life. For God sent not his Son into the world to condemn the world; but that the world through him might be saved. He that believeth on him is not condemned: but he that believeth not is condemned already, because he hath not believed in the name of the only begotten Son of God."*

This section of scripture tells us God's purpose for giving His son Jesus to the world. The world was in a bad condition. The world was overwrought with sin; the people were living for fleshly desires rather than for God's desires.

As a result of the world's conditions, God decided He would offer the perfect sacrifice that would save the world from being a place where people were lost and had no hope. He decided that His own son could stand in proxy for the sin-filled world, taking all sin upon Himself.

So Jesus came, born of a virgin, to save this dying world. He walked on this earth for 33 ½ years, doing the work of His Heavenly Father. At the appointed time, He died by way of crucifixion upon a cross at Calvary, on Golgatha's hill. He shed his blood and died for you and for me. Because His blood was pure, it paid the penalty for all unrighteousness and gave those who believe in Him direct access to His father's throne.

Scripture tells us in Matthew 27:51 that the veil of the temple was ripped in two from top to bottom, at the moment that Jesus' spirit left His body. As a result of the veil's removal, we are no longer required to have a high priest make intercession for us. We, as the children of the Most High God, are able to approach the throne God for ourselves, and Jesus sits on the right hand of the Father making intercession for us.

But what is even more miraculous than God offering His own son as the perfect sacrifice was the fact that when Jesus was placed in grave clothes and placed in a tomb, He only remained there until the third day. God would not have it that His son would remain in the heart of the earth forever. In order for people to believe in the awesome power of God and His dear son Jesus, a miracle had to be performed. So, on the third day, after Jesus died on the cross, He was resurrected, demonstrating the omnipotence of God. This very act was the act that would cause people to believe in a god that reigns supreme and holds the power of the universe in His very hands, a god that could save them from themselves.

Today, if you are an unbeliever, you can change your destiny. You can change where you will spend your eternity. Our Heavenly Father gives us the freedom of choice about how we want to live our life here on earth and how we want to spend eternity. In Deuteronomy 30:19, God boldly declares, *"I call heaven and earth to record this day against you, that I have set before you life and death, blessing and cursing: therefore choose life, that both thou and thy seed may live."*

So, dear friend what choice will you make today? Will you spend your eternity with the Creator or will you suffer Hell's eternal flames? Again, the choice is yours. Just as the men aboard the ship who were with Jonah became believers, you too can make a choice to accept the only one and true living God as your god.

If after reading the above passages, you have decided that you want to spend your eternity in Heaven with God, the creator, and His son Jesus, and the Holy Spirit, read through what has affectionately come to be known as the Roman's Road. This is the road to salvation. As you read through the scriptures that comprise the Roman's Road, you will also read the explanation for each scripture so you will have clarity about what you are reading and confessing.

The Roman's Road to Salvation

The road to salvation begins with Romans 3:23 which declares, *"For all have sinned, and come short of the glory of God."* This scripture explains that everyone has come short of God's glory and needs redemption. Then Romans 6:23a states, *"For the wages of sin is death."* Here, we learn that the consequence of living a life of sin is death. Everyone will experience physical death as a result of the sin committed in the garden of Eden, but those who commit themselves to a life of sin will suffer eternal damnation in the lake of fire (Rev. 19).

Continue with the rest of verse 6:23 that says, *"but the gift of God is eternal life through Jesus Christ our Lord."* There is an alternative to suffering eternal damnation. We can accept the gift of salvation by accepting Jesus as our personal lord and savior. Then, Romans 5:8 says, *"But God commendeth his love toward us, in that, while we were yet sinners, Christ died for us."* We are able to receive the gift of salvation because Christ came to earth and shed His blood for us on the cross.

Continue to Romans 10: 9-10 which says, *"That if thou shalt confess with thy mouth the Lord Jesus, and shalt believe in thine heart that God hath raised him from the dead, thou shalt be saved. For with the heart man believeth unto righteousness; and with the mouth confession is made unto salvation."* If we confess with our mouths that Jesus is the son of God, that he came and died for our sins, and that God raised Him from the dead, we will receive salvation.

Finish with Romans 10:13, which states, *"For whosoever shall call upon the name of the Lord shall be saved."* Call upon the name of God by saying these words, **"Lord Jesus, come into my heart and save me Lord. I believe that you are the Son of God who came and died on the cross for my sins. I believe that you rose from the grave. I also believe that you now sit in heaven on the right side of** the Father, making intersession for me. I accept you as my Lord and my Savior."

Now that you have confessed with your mouth that Jesus is the son of God and that He died for our sins and rose from the grave, **YOU ARE NOW SAVED!!!!** You will spend your eternity in heaven.

The next step is very important- you must find a Bible-based church that teaches the word of God and confesses the Lord Jesus Christ to be the son of God. Don't delay. Do this immediately. Do not leave yourself open to the enemy. Get connected with the saints of the Most High God and keep yourself covered with the unspotted blood of the lamb.

Here is my prayer for you.
Father God,

I thank you for the opportunity to minister your word to the unsaved, the unchurched, and the uncommitted. Father God, I pray now for the souls who have just received the gift of salvation. Lord Father, they have opened their hearts to you, and I know that you have received them into your kingdom and written their names in the Book of Life. Father God, I pray that you will touch their lives and show yourself mightily before them. Let their eyes be opened by the scales falling off, allowing them to see clearly.

Father God, I even pray for the backslider, those who have turned away from you after receiving the gift of salvation. You said in your word that you desire that none would perish. So Lord, I send your word to them right now praying that they would confess the iniquity in their heart, repent, and turn from their evil ways, so that they may receive a life of abundance. You said in your word in Matthew Chapter 14, that every knee shall bow before you and every tongue will confess that Jesus is Lord.

Father God, I pray now that we all come under subjection to your word and that we will humbly submit our lives to you. I ask all these things in the name of my Lord and Savior Jesus Christ. Amen, Amen, Amen!!!!

I will continue to pray for your success in your walk with God. Remember, this spiritual walk that you are about to embark on will not be an easy walk, but remember, the race is not given to the swift but to those who endure to the end.

Be blessed with heaven's best. I love you!

References

Gill, John. *John Gill's Exposition of the Bible.* *http://www.biblestudytools.com/commentaries/gills-exposition-of-the-bible/*

Taber, Duke. "How To Boldly Go Into Your Next Spiritual Assignment"
https://www.viralbeliever.com/bible-studies/how-to-boldly-go-into-your-next-spiritual-assignment.

About the Author

Dr. Cassundra White-Elliott resides in California with her family, where as an English/Education professor she works for various community colleges and universities.

When writing, she writes with the direction of the Holy Spirit, in an effort to share with God's people all that He has for them.

In addition to teaching and writing, Dr. White-Elliott also serves as an evangelistic teacher. She is also the founder of International Women's Commission, a ministry that serves the needs of the entire person, by attending to healing the mind, body, soul, and spirit.

Dr. White-Elliott holds a Ph.D. in Education, a Master's in English Composition, and a Bachelor's in Education.

Dr. White-Elliott is also the founder of CLF Publishing, LLC. For your publishing needs, go online to www.clfpublishing.org.

OTHER BOOKS BY THE AUTHOR
(All books can be purchased at www.creativemindsbookstore.com)

From Despair, through Determination, to Victory!

A lot can happen during a span of 40 years. The life of Dr. Cassundra White-Elliott has been anything but uneventful. From a fun-loving childhood sprinkled with incidents of abuse to a tumultuous young adulthood to a stable, secure adult life, she has experienced a full life, with much more to come. Her story is inspiring and motivating.

If anyone lacks hope, reading Dr. White-Elliott's autobiography will propel him/her into attitude of "Maybe I can." This attitude, if nurtured and developed, will grow into an attitude of "Yes, I can." Throughout her life, Cassundra has always held in her heart the belief that she could achieve anything that she had a made-up mind to embark upon. She was determined to achieve her heart's desires, doing what God has called her to do. She takes no credit for herself. All the glory goes to God, for He is her driving force. In Him, she lives, moves, and has her being.

Through the Storm

Through the Storm was duly inspired by the avaricious cloud of depression that decided to hover overhead of my daily existence in the latter part of 2007. Although I found it extremely difficult, I was once again compelled to not be defeated by just another snare that the enemy, the trickster, set for me. Once again, or more appropriately I should say *continuously*, he has exerted pernicious efforts to snatch the very life out of me by causing me to wallow in despair and to believe that I had been overcome by failure when in actuality and all reality, I was just experiencing a temporary setback. During those cloudy days, I had to remind myself daily that even though I was a target of the enemy, I am and will always be a child of the Most High god, Jehovah, who is my rock, my stability.

Unleashed Anger, Anger Unleashed

Introduction
What Is This Book All About?

As I prepared to embark upon the adventure of writing this book, I had to prepare myself to also be transparent. I have found that being transparent is required in order for healing to transpire, healing for all those that peruse the pages of this book and myself. And I may as well tell you that today, at the onset of this project, I have not been totally delivered from my condition of being an anger-filled person. However, I am definitely a work in progress. I have made strides with the assistance of my Lord and Savior, Jesus Christ, who is the head of my life. Without his love, guidance, and teachings, I would not be the woman of God I am today. I shudder to think where I could be instead and will therefore not entertain the thought.

Public Speaking in the Spiritual Arena

Chapter Two
How Communication Works
Purpose: This chapter will explain the six primary components of communication, identifying their purpose and how they work together.

<u>The Source</u>

In oral communication, the source of information is the speaker. In a church setting, the foundation of the message is God's word, but it is a speaker's interpretation of God's word that is delivered to the audience. As speakers vary, the information may vary but should have a similar essence because the foundational text is the same.

<u>The Message</u>

The message is the collective set of ideas that the speaker (the source) wants to deliver and/or illustrate to the audience. The message can be informative where the speaker informs the audience about a specific set of information. Or, the message may be persuasive in nature if the speaker wants to persuade the audience about conducting themselves in a specific manner, accepting God's commandments, or any number of things.

Where is Your Joppa?

Introduction

Where is Your Joppa? was written for the express purpose of illustrating God's call for obedience in the lives of believers with respect to the individual call that He has on each of our lives. As you read throughout the various chapters, notice that the emphasis is placed on our persistent disobedience in answering God's call in a specific area of our lives. We have become a people who are similar to the Israelites when they found themselves in the middle of the wilderness, following their exodus from Egypt. Before God, they murmured and complained about their current life conditions and failed to be obedient to God's statutes delivered through His servant Moses. Their persistent disobedience caused them to lose the opportunity to see and enter the Promised Land. I ask you, "What has your disobedience cost you?" "Was your disobedience worth what it cost you?" "Do you think about the souls you could have ushered into the kingdom of God?" These are some of the questions that I pray will be answered through your reading of the book.

Mayhem in the Hamptons

Romero and Yolanda optimistically plan for the day that is going to change their lives from being single persons to a couple who is united in holy matrimony. They, along with their parents, close friends and family, fly over to the infamous Hamptons, where only the rich and famous vacation, to have their dream wedding at the five-star Hampton Suites located on a peninsula in the Hamptons. Little do they know that their perfect day will turn out to be less than perfect when their wedding planner Mariesha Coleman suddenly goes missing!

A time when the newlyweds' lives should be filled with joy and the creation of wonderful memories, they are stricken with grief as they desperately try to find clues to help solve Mariesha's disappearance.

Mayhem in the Hamptons is a tale that shares how the horrors of a woman's past can come back to haunt her in more than one way and the impact it can have on anyone who gets in the way.

Preacher's Daughter

Tinisha, the daughter of a preacher, is a twenty-six year old God-fearing young woman endeavoring to complete law school so that she can make her mark in the courtroom. Working in one of the late-night clubs in Hollywood to earn money to pay her own way through school, Tinisha soon learns that life doesn't always go as planned. Finding her strength in her faith, Tinisha constantly finds herself praying as she watches God move miraculously in her life.

Preacher's Son

    Romero Turner is a private investigator with a promising future. As he continues to build his career, he is excited about the cases he undertakes. However, his father Pastor Theodore Turner has other plans for his son's life. In the midst of trying to save his client's husband from Sylvester Domingo, a ruthless crime lord, Romero must try to salvage his relationship with his father. He must decide if ministry or life as a detective is in his future.

Lord, Teach Me to be a Blessing!

Lord, Teach Me to be a Blessing! will change a person's mentality from being centered around "me, myself, and I" to focusing on "others."

The world system teaches us that it is acceptable to place ourselves above others in an attempt to get ahead and even to survive. Herbert Spencer coined the phrase *'survival of the fittest'* after reading Charles Darwin's theory of evolution. This concept of surpassing and outdoing others is the world's philosophy.

However, the word of God does not subscribe to or promote this self-centered ideology, and therefore, neither should believers. We must hold fast to the truths outlined in Holy Scripture: *"Love thy neighbor as you love thyself"* (James 2:8) and *"It is more blessed to give than to receive"* (Acts 20:35).

While holding God's truths to be self-evident, we must demonstrate them to others, thereby showing them the way of the Lord of how to be a blessing to someone *rather* than looking to receive a blessing.

This is the very purpose of this book: to change the mentality of the world from being *self*-centered to *other* centered.

After the Dust Settles

Throughout the journey of life, we all experience ups and downs and joys and pains. Most of us successfully find solutions to the situations/problems we encounter, but we often avoid dealing with the attached emotions. If we continue to ignore the emotions of pain, hurt, disappointment, anger, etc., we set ourselves up for destruction. Our families, our cultures, and our society tell us to be strong, to keep our chin up, and to grin and bear it. However, these methods of avoidance can lead us to strokes due to the undue amount of pressure we place on ourselves and/or mental illness from being unable to cope with the emotional baggage we have accumulated.

In *After the Dust Settles,* Dr. C. White-Elliott shares several situations that we all may encounter at one time or another in our lifetime and how to successfully navigate through them, so we can find ourselves emotionally healthy after the dust has settled and the situation has been rectified.

Begin reading today and experience a better tomorrow!

A Diamond in the Rough

A Diamond in the Rough Architecture Firm was built and is owned and operated by lead architect Kyra Fraser. For the last five years, Kyra has been extremely successful in business, but her love life leaves much to be desired.

Kyra has set high standards for herself and does not wish to take a man in any condition and attempt to make him over. She is looking for someone who is drama free, well educated, very cultured, fun-loving, good looking, self-motivated, and the list goes on.

Will Kyra find the man of her dreams, or will her dream just continue to be a dream?

As you delve into this page-turning novel, Kyra's reality will unfold as you are drawn into her world of design, love and office drama- which includes her best friend's husband who is looking for love in all the wrong places.

365 Days of Encouragement

Just as our brain requires oxygen obtained from the air we breathe to sustain our mortal bodies, our spirit requires revitalization and encouragement in order to be strengthened each and every day of our lives. The revitalization and encouragement needed for the spirit of man comes directly from the word of God and assists us in walking according to the way of our heavenly Father. 365 Days of Encouragement provides a scripture a day for each day of the year. Along with the daily scripture is a brief note of commentary also for the benefit of edifying the saints of God.

It is my prayer that the people of God would live a fulfilled life through Christ Jesus. Knowing His word and understanding we can walk in the fulfillment thereof is empowering. We are instructed in II Timothy 2:15, "Study to shew thyself approved unto God, a workman that needeth not to be ashamed, rightly dividing the word of truth" (KJV). Take an opportunity to delve further into the word of God, to know His statutes and to allow your own personal life to be edified, so you can be equipped to bring glory to God and lived a fulfilled life.

A Mother's Heart

A Mother's Heart shares the unconditional love of mothers through a compilation of testimonies. Each testimony serves as a tribute to a special mother. The children of the represented mothers have lovingly written about their childhood, young adult life and/or older adult experiences they shared with their mother. As you read the writers' reflections, you will feel the expressions of love exude from the pages.

The purpose of this book is two-fold. First, it honors those mothers who stood by their children through the trials of life and showered them with unconditional love. Second, the book is a source of encouragement for mothers who may feel inadequate and question whether or not they are actually suited for motherhood. Our advice to mothers is, "Be encouraged; the journey of motherhood may seem daunting at times and you may shed some tears, but your children will never forget the love you have shown them and instilled in them to share with others."

Mothers may not be perfect, but they are definitely unmatched by any other category of person on God's green earth!

Broken Chains

Broken Chains is an in-depth survey of five life-changing tragedies that can and will serve as chains to bind us if we are not watchful and mindful of their potential effects. In our lifetimes, we may all experience death of loved ones, sexual abuse, broken relationships, promiscuity, and sickness and disease. These everyday life occurrences can have detrimental effects on the remaining years of our lives and change our existence, unless we deal with them in a healthy manner.

Broken Chains not only brings to light the detrimental effects of five life-changing tragedies, but it also shares how anyone who experiences them can be healed and delivered from their effects.

If you have experienced death of a loved one, sexual abuse, a broken relationship, the effects of promiscuity, and/or sickness and disease and have not been able to rid yourself of the emotions attached to them or specific resulting behaviors, Broken Chains is for you.

God designed each of us for a purpose, and He has an intended end for us to achieve. In order for us to effectively achieve our God-given purpose, we must be free of chains that bind us. It is not God's desire that we become immobilized by life's events. His desire is for us to be healed, delivered and set free. Be healed today, in the name of the Lord Jesus Christ!

I Have Fallen

Do you know anyone who has committed his/her life to Christ but has done something unseemly that you would never expect a Christian to do? How did you feel about that person or what the person did? Did you pass judgment? What if that person were you? How would you feel if you made a misstep and no one forgave you and instead began to treat you differently? How do you feel when you are judged for past mistakes or lifestyles that are no longer part of your life?

This book shares four true stories of Christians who have made missteps during their walk with God. The purpose is not to air their dirty laundry, but to demonstrate our humanness and our vulnerability. None of us are exempt from making errors and falling into sin. It can happen to any of us.

The solution for these dilemmas is for the person who fell into sin to make a life-changing move and turn away from the sin, repent and ask God for forgiveness. His arms are waiting!

The next solution is for those who witness the sin or know of it. Pray and be of comfort to the one who has fallen. Lead him/her back to the path of righteousness. Love thy neighbor and treat him/her as you want to be treated!

The Bottom Line

The Bottom Line is a detailed review of the Book of Job. Much can be said about Job's experiences with the loss of his children and wealth and the subsequent return of it all in mass proportions. However, the telling of Job's story in the Holy writ was not intended to focus on the return of his wealth. Instead, the focal point should be on the bottom line of the entire situation.

When you experience trials or tragedies in your life, do you tend to focus on the trial itself, the result, or the bottom line?

"What is the bottom line?" you may ask. The bottom line is the message God is sending regarding the situation.

When Job experienced his tragedies, there was a bottom line. Likewise, when you experience your trials and tragedies, there is a bottom line as well. It is up to you to discover it.

This book will reveal the bottom line in the Book of Job. It is readily apparent, but many often overlook it.

Now, it is up to you to uncover the bottom line of your experiences, for God will not bring a trial to you without a good reason.

Power of a Woman

The ongoing conversation about the value of a woman is presented from a different perspective in The Power of a Woman. Dr. Cassundra White-Elliott presents a biblical perspective of women and compares it to the worldview of both yesterday and today. This comparison seeks to illustrate God's intended purpose for His uniquely designed creation: woman. Dr. Elliott shares God's truth about pre-imposed limitations set by man versus the limitations God Himself set for woman in addition to the wealth of liberality He gave her.

Women's creativity and abilities are not meant to be stifled. They are meant to be utilized to bring glory to God, to help sustain and nurture their families, and to move the world forward. Knowing God's truth will show women how to celebrate and appreciate who they are as well as one another!

Women, let's take the blinders off, lift our heads up, and march forward, side by side with men, and bring glory and honor to God! Take your rightful place with a gentle smile and grace and be who God called you to be!

Set Free

If you possess habits and display characteristics that are unbecoming, debilitating, and hinder the desired progress in your life or that affect your relationships with others, Set Free will provide the steps you need to be healed and delivered, through the Word of God. Deliverance is available to you! Claim your healing today and walk in victory!

Do You Know God?

Have you or someone you know ever felt alone, confused, or unsure about your walk with God or are you unsure of what being a Christian is all about? *Do You Know God?* is an excellent text for providing answers to many of your questions. This book introduces adolescents and young adults to God in addition to answer many of their questions about being a Christian. This book shares the testimonies of the trials and tribulations that other teens have experienced and how God prevailed in their lives. All the information that is shared on the pages of the book is based upon the Word of God and the scriptures are taken from the King James Version of the Bible. If you are interested in knowing more about God's Word or how to begin your Christian experience, this book is for you.

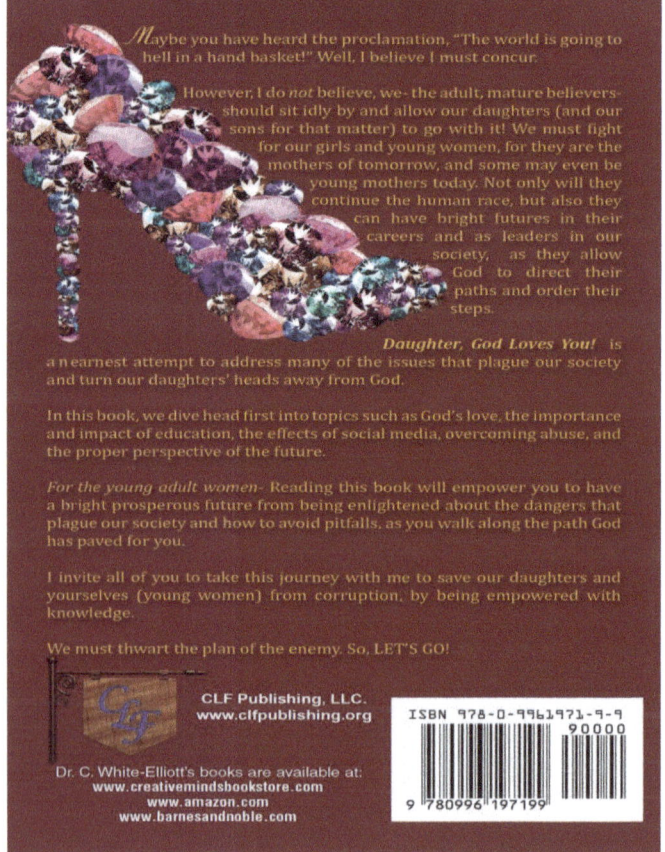

Time is Running Out!

A Mother's Heart II shares the unconditional love of mothers through a compilation of testimonies. Each testimony serves as a tribute to a special mother. The children of the represented mothers have lovingly written about their childhood, young adult life and/or older adult experiences they shared with their mother. As you read the writers' reflections, you will feel the expressions of love exude from the pages.

The purpose of this book is two-fold. First, it honors those mothers who stood by their children through the trials of life and showered them with unconditional love. Second, the book is a source of encouragement for mothers who may feel inadequate and question whether or not they are actually suited for motherhood. Our advice to mothers is, *"Be encouraged; the journey of motherhood may seem daunting at times and you may shed some tears, but your children will never forget the love you have shown them and instilled in them to share with others."*

Mothers may not be perfect, but they are definitely unmatched by any other category of person on God's green earth!

The following authors are included in this compilation:
Edwin Baltierra, Shelia Bryant-Colbert, Jean Cedeno,
Ilse Guadalupe Hernandez, Haley Keil, Haley King, Johnathon Lopez,
Ronnette Moore, Allyson Marie Sanders, Lucas van den Elzen,
Daron C. White, Ashton Wilson, Jessica Yslas, and Vanessa Zavala

CLF Publishing, LLC.
www.clfpublishing.org

Dr. Cassundra White-Elliott's books are available at:
www.creativemindsbookstore.com
www.amazon.com
www.barnesandnoble.com

Dr. C. White-Elliott

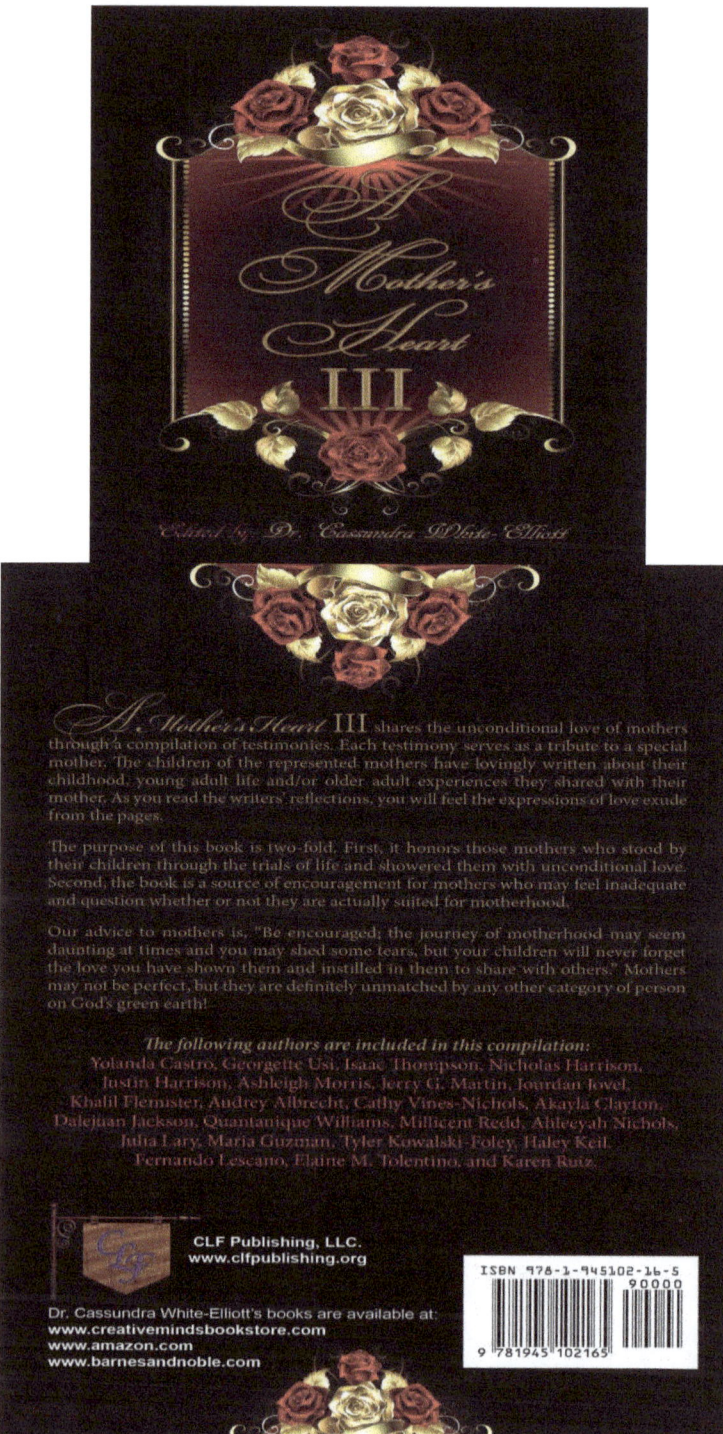

A year ago, Charlito Jimenez was found in his den, lying on the couch, with a fatal gunshot wound in his temple. Everyone in the community still wants to know who is guilty of the unfathomable crime.

Tinisha Salisbury, attorney at law, has taken the case of the accused. Can she prove her client's innocence or will a guilty verdict be rendered?

Halfway through the trial, a badly burned body was found at the scene of a fire.

Is there a string of murders being committed?

Are the murders related?

Web of Lies spins the tales of several characters into one web. Each has a story to tell, and everyone has something to hide. The web of lies, deceit, and revenge take over the lives of these characters to the point where they may not be able to see their way clear.

CLF Publishing, LLC.
www.clfpublishing.org

ISBN 978-1-945102-20-2

Dr. C. White-Elliott's books are available at:
www.creativemindsbookstore.com
www.amazon.com
www.barnesandnoble.com

www.ingramcontent.com/pod-product-compliance
Lightning Source LLC
Chambersburg PA
CBHW041925090426
42743CB00020B/3447